A FUNDER'S GUIDE TO
Organizational Assessment

Tools, Processes, and Their Use in Building Capacity

EDITOR
Lori Bartczak, Grantmakers for Effective Organizations

CONTRIBUTORS

Kevin Bolduc

Phil Buchanan

Stephanie Clohesy

Kathie deNobriga

Dorothy Freeman

Kendall Guthrie

Maria Gutierrez

Judy Huang

Sandra Jacobsen

Carol Lukas

Daraus Mirza

Alan Preston

Lori Roming

Gladys Washington

FIELDSTONE
ALLIANCE

SAINT PAUL
MINNESOTA

We thank the David and Lucile Packard Foundation for its support of this publication.

Fieldstone Alliance is committed to strengthening the performance of the nonprofit sector. Through the synergy of its consulting, training, publishing, and research and demonstration projects, Fieldstone Alliance provides solutions to issues facing nonprofits, funders, and the communities they serve. Fieldstone Alliance was formerly Wilder Publishing and Wilder Consulting departments of the Amherst H. Wilder Foundation. If you would like more information about Fieldstone Alliance and our services, please contact Fieldstone Alliance, 60 Plato Boulevard East, Suite 150, Saint Paul, MN 55107, 651-556-4500.

We hope you find this book useful! For information about other Fieldstone Alliance publications, please see the ordering information on the last page or contact:

Fieldstone Alliance Publishing Center
60 Plato Boulevard East
Suite 150
Saint Paul, MN 55107
800-274-6024
www.FieldstoneAlliance.org

Edited by Lori Bartczak and Vince Hyman
Designed by Kirsten Nielsen
Cover designed by Rebecca Andrews

Manufactured in the United States
First Printing, December 2005

Library of Congress Cataloging-in-Publication Data

A funder's guide to organizational assessment : tools, processes, and their use in building capacity / contributors, Kevin Bolduc ... [et al.] ; [edited by] Lori Bartczak.-- 1st ed.
    p. cm.
 Includes index.
 ISBN-13: 978-0-940069-53-4
 ISBN-10: 0-940069-53-9
 1. Nonprofit organizations--Evaluation. 2. Nonprofit organizations--Finance. 3. Organizational effectiveness--Evaluation--Methodology. 4. Nonprofit organizations--United States. I. Bolduc, Kevin. II. Bartczak, Lori, 1977-
 HD2769.15.F857 2005
 658.4'013--dc22

2005030205

A FUNDER'S GUIDE *from*
Fieldstone Alliance & GEO

A Funder's Guide to Organizational Assessment is one of a series of works published by Fieldstone Alliance in collaboration with Grantmakers for Effective Organizations (GEO). Together, we hope to strengthen nonprofit organizations, the communities they serve, and the nonprofit sector by helping grantmakers in their work with nonprofits.

Other books in this series:

Strengthening Nonprofit Performance: A Funder's Guide to Capacity Building by Paul Connolly and Carol Lukas

Community Visions, Community Solutions: Grantmaking for Comprehensive Impact by Joseph A. Connor and Stephanie Kadel-Taras

A Funder's Guide to Evaluation: Leveraging Evaluation to Improve Nonprofit Effectiveness by Peter York

A Funder's Guide to Public Policy (working title), edited by David F. Arons (available in 2006)

About Grantmakers for Effective Organizations

Grantmakers for Effective Organizations (GEO) is a coalition of more than five hundred grantmakers committed to building strong and effective nonprofit organizations. GEO's mission is to maximize philanthropy's impact by advancing the effectiveness of grantmakers and their grantees. The organization does this by

- Commissioning and contributing to research

- Developing programs and products

- Building a community of practice that expands the resources available on nonprofit effectiveness

More information on GEO and a host of resources and links for funders are available at www.geofunders.org.

About Fieldstone Alliance

Fieldstone Alliance is a nonprofit organization with a mission to strengthen the performance of the nonprofit sector. Through the synergy of its consulting, training, publishing, and research and demonstration projects, Fieldstone Alliance provides solutions to issues facing nonprofits, funders, and the communities they serve. The staff of Fieldstone Alliance bring passion, commitment, and focus to deliver the effective results their partners expect. Fieldstone Alliance was formerly Wilder Publishing and Wilder Consulting, both departments of the Amherst H. Wilder Foundation.

Learn more about Fieldstone Alliance at www.FieldstoneAlliance.org.

About the Contributors

Introduction

SANDRA JACOBSEN is a managing consultant with Fieldstone Alliance. She has more than twenty-five years of experience in leadership development, capacity building, and organizational transitions in both for-profit and nonprofit organizations. For twenty years, Sandy was in a leadership position in the financial services industry, working with corporate, nonprofit, and government clients throughout the United States. She served as president of two banks and launched a national community development initiative. Recognizing the great need to share successful strategies between the sectors, Sandy transitioned to the nonprofit sector and stepped in as interim director of a nonprofit housing organization. She is able to apply her extensive practical experience and academic training to almost any challenge leaders and their organizations face. Sandy has degrees in economics and psychology.

CAROL LUKAS is president of Fieldstone Alliance and former director of National Services for Amherst H. Wilder Foundation. She has been executive director of nonprofit organizations, a trustee of a community foundation, a consultant in a Fortune 500 company, and a small business owner. She has more than twenty-five years of consulting and training experience with nonprofits, government, foundations, businesses, and collaboratives. Carol focuses on building the capacity of national networks and organizations and on strengthening connections between the public, private, and nonprofit sectors as they address urban issues. She specializes in helping organizations and collaboratives plan and manage change in strategic direction and organization structure and capacity. She is author and coauthor of *Consulting with Non-profits: A Practitioner's Guide, Strengthening Nonprofit Performance: A Funder's Guide to Capacity Building,* and *Conducting Community Forums.*

Chapter 1

KENDALL GUTHRIE is vice president for strategy at Blueprint Research & Design, Inc. She helps grantmakers develop systems to assess the effectiveness of their grantmaking strategies and refine their program designs. She has expertise in both qualitative and quantitative research methods, including surveys, focus groups, interviews, content analysis, and case studies. She also has twelve years of experience researching, designing, and operating programs to help nonprofits and government agencies develop innovative applications of information technology. Before joining Blueprint, Kendall worked as deputy director of HandsNet, a national nonprofit technology assistance organization, and as director of telecommunications planning for the City of New York. Kendall holds a bachelor's degree from Duke University and a PhD from the Annenberg School for Communications at the University of Southern California.

ALAN PRESTON, senior analyst at Blueprint Research & Design, has extensive leadership and management experience in the nonprofit sector as a program manager, board member, and consultant. He also has specialized training from the Peter Drucker Foundation in strategic planning and outcome evaluation. He has a specific expertise in workforce development issues. Alan has been involved with several philanthropic foundations in Seattle, serves as a board member of Powerful Schools, and brings to Blueprint a passion for leveraging philanthropy to affect social change. He holds a bachelor's degree in political science from Haverford College and an MBA from the JL Kellogg Graduate School of Management at Northwestern University.

Chapter 2

MARIA GUTIERREZ is the vice president for organizational development and a ten-year veteran of the Local Initiatives Support Corporation (LISC). Maria leads LISC's Organizational Development Initiative (ODI), an in-house management consulting, technical assistance, and training division, and has been responsible for the development of many of its innovative consulting and intervention methodologies, as well as the creation of numerous tools and resources for the community development industry.

DARAUS MIRZA is a senior program officer in LISC's ODI and leads the Capacity Mapping Project. Daraus is also responsible for all of ODI's board governance programming and the creation of a number of highly acclaimed training and technical assistance resources for CDC staff and boards.

Chapter 3

DOROTHY (DOTT) FREEMAN was named president of the Unity Foundation in October 2001 and held that post until February 2005. Freeman's applied research interests and the Unity Foundation's venture philanthropy mission led to the design and testing of C.Q.® (Capacity Quotient)—a strategic tool for assessing capacity and formulating fundable plans for capacity-building tied to C.Q. Freeman's twenty-five-year career in philanthropy, nonprofit management, and higher education includes senior foundation and institutional advancement posts in New England and the Midwest. Prior to joining the Unity Foundation during its establishment, she served as executive director of the Johnson Center for Philanthropy and Nonprofit Leadership at Grand Valley State University in Grand Rapids, Michigan, where she was also on the graduate faculty in the School of Public and Nonprofit Management. Freeman also served as a board member for the Direction Center—a W. K. Kellogg-funded management support organization in West Michigan. Freeman holds bachelor's and master's degrees from Ball State University and a PhD from Indiana University.

LORI ROMING joined the Unity Foundation in 2001 as an administrative assistant and was promoted to the post of research and program officer in 2003. Roming manages the administration of charitable grants to 501(c)(3) nonprofit organizations, facilitates Unity Foundation projects, and coordinates national research efforts in benchmarking and building the management capacity of nonprofits in education, arts, environment, at-risk youth, and community and economic development. During her long and varied working life, Roming has worked for the federal government, private industry, and nonprofit organizations. All of her experiences are put to good use at the Unity Foundation. She actively participates in community nonprofits as well as continuing her education.

Chapter 4

KATHIE deNOBRIGA grew up in Kingsport, Tennessee. For a dozen years she directed and produced community and children's theatre and managed a performing arts center in North Carolina. She also toured with the Road Company for three years as a member of the creative ensemble. A founding member of Alternate ROOTS, deNobriga served as ROOTS' director for ten years. She is now an independent arts consultant.

GLADYS WASHINGTON is senior program officer of the Mary Reynolds Babcock Foundation in Winston-Salem, North Carolina. She manages the Community Problem Solving and Grassroots Leadership Development Programs. Before coming to the Babcock Foundation in 1999, Gladys was a Program Officer for the Community Foundation Serving Coastal South Carolina in Charleston. Gladys holds degrees from the College of Charleston and the Universities of Charleston and South Carolina. She has four children and three grandchildren. She is a member of Union Baptist Church in Winston-Salem, North Carolina.

Chapter 5

PHIL BUCHANAN, executive director of the Center for Effective Philanthropy, was the first staff member hired in August 2001. At the Center, Phil has built a research team, secured funding, developed a research and education agenda, and managed the development and introduction of new performance assessment tools, including the Grantee Perception Report. He led the Center's Foundation Performance Metrics Pilot Study as well as the first phase of the Center's Foundation Governance Project. Phil speaks regularly at national and regional gatherings of foundation and nonprofit executives and trustees on issues of foundation effectiveness, foundation–grantee relations, foundation governance, and assessment of foundation performance. He has experience in strategy consulting as a principal at the Parthenon Group where he worked with senior executives at a variety of companies to define strategies and assess performance. He also has significant nonprofit management experience at Wesleyan University, where he served as special assistant to the president, and Mount Holyoke College, where he was assistant to the president and also secretary of the college. His writings on educational and management issues have appeared in the *New York Times,* the *Boston Globe, Foundation News and Commentary,* and the *Chronicle of Higher Education,* among other publications. He received his undergraduate degree in government from Wesleyan University and holds an MBA from Harvard University.

KEVIN BOLDUC, associate director at the Center for Effective Philanthropy, works extensively on the design and execution of research on overall foundation performance assessment. Kevin leads the center's ongoing studies of grantee perceptions of foundations, including the execution and analysis of the center's biannual comparative surveys of foundation grantees. He has created and presented Grantee Perception Reports for dozens of foundations, conducted focus groups, and spoken about this work at gatherings of foundation and nonprofit executives. Kevin also coauthored the first in a series of case studies that highlight effective and innovative practices, and is currently overseeing the pilot of a comparative survey of foundation staff. Kevin also has a variety of responsibilities related to the management of the center and its budget. Prior to joining the center in September 2001, Kevin was a consultant with the Parthenon Group, a Boston-based strategy consulting firm. He graduated summa cum laude with bachelor's degree in biology from Williams College.

JUDY HUANG, senior research analyst at the Center for Effective Philanthropy, is primarily involved in the analysis of grantee survey data and has presented results of the Grantee Perception Report to dozens of foundation boards and staffs. She also helped create the Applicant Perception Report and has conducted focus groups of nonprofits to further explore the center's findings on the foundation–nonprofit relationship. In addition, she has worked to gather and analyze operational benchmarking data for foundations and has a number of ongoing responsibilities related to the center's communications efforts. Prior to joining the center in September 2002, Judy was a consultant with Alliance Consulting Group, a Boston-based strategy consulting firm. She is also cofounder of the DREAM Program, a nonprofit children's mentoring and service organization based in Vermont. Judy has a bachelor's degree in English modified with history from Dartmouth College.

Chapter 6

STEPHANIE J. CLOHESY is the founder and principal of Clohesy Consulting, an organizational development firm offering a broad variety of planning, research, and design services to philanthropic foundations and to national and international nonprofit institutions. Stephanie's thirty years of national and international experiences include work on public policy reform, women's and human rights, civic participation and democratization, and organizational and leadership development.

Stephanie's recent developmental and research work in philanthropy has helped launch several new foundations and programs while also contributing to the formation of a future agenda for philanthropy and nonprofits in online and knowledge-based systems.

Contents

Foreword

In today's world of modern conveniences, many problems can be solved more quickly with the use of various assessment tools. If one's car is not running as it should, a mechanic will run a diagnostic to determine the root of the problem. High school students who are sorting through college and career options with uncertainty can take a test to help them identify career paths for which they might be well suited. Many individuals today can tell you their IQ, their body mass index rating, their credit rating, or their Briggs-Meyer personality type—all commonly accepted assessments of individual intelligence, health, financial reliability, or character.

The use of assessment tools has taken hold in the philanthropic sector as well. An increasing number of grantmakers are creating, modifying, or adopting assessment tools that can identify capacity strengths and weaknesses of both grantee and grantmaking organizations.

This book is written primarily for grantmakers who are aware of the benefits of providing capacity-building support and are interested in learning how capacity assessment tools can strengthen their work with grantees. The book has two parts, which are prefaced by an introduction (and warning) on the powerful consequences of organizational assessment. Part 1 provides examples of grantmakers' efforts to assess grantee performance using a variety of tools. Part 2 provides examples and tools grantmakers can use to assess their own activities—a wise place for them to begin, as suggested in the book's conclusion. Additionally, a CD provides examples of tools grantmakers can use to assess their own effectiveness.

Assessment Is a Powerful Change Strategy

by Carol Lukas and Sandra Jacobsen, Fieldstone Alliance

The growing need in our society for the critical services nonprofits offer leads us to an inevitable conclusion: it is only through building the capacity of nonprofits that we can meet those needs and strengthen civil society. Funders who work with nonprofits to build their capacity can be a powerful force for change, both for the nonprofits and for the communities they serve. Unfortunately, many nonprofits are underresourced and underperforming. Most nonprofits will quickly say that their greatest need is for more money. Yet funders know that money is often not the solution. Nonprofits need smarter and more strategic ways of operating if they hope to survive in a competitive environment. They need to be more agile in responding to rapidly changing demographics, technologies, and markets. They need stronger leadership to make difficult decisions. They need help shoring up their organizations to support the rapid changes required of their programs and to ensure that they are achieving the desired impact in the world.

Organizational assessment, at its best, is a positive, constructive step toward health and improved performance for any organization. It allows organizations to step back and take stock of where they are in their development, what their strengths and challenges are, and the choices they need to make for future success. Assessment can make it possible for organizations to learn how they are performing compared to their peers—other organizations in a similar industry or community. Assessment can be the launching point for a planned change effort—whether it is strategic planning, restructuring, program development, service delivery enhancements, or targeted organizational improvements. Assessment can motivate a sluggish board, or help a funder make wise funding decisions. At its best, assessment can deliver all of these benefits.

This book is organized into two parts. Part 1 describes four richly varied approaches to organizational assessment, each one tailored to fit the grantmaking organization's goals, the needs and challenges of the nonprofits it supports, and the resources available or needed in their community. Because grantmakers cannot help grantees build capacity without critically assessing their *own* capacity, Part 2 highlights two tools for assessing grantmaker capacity. By providing these examples, this book aims to help grantmakers sort through the issues one must consider when designing a capacity assessment instrument, with hopes that grantmakers can learn from the experiences of their colleagues.

As you read these examples you might ask, Why did they choose to do it that way? or Could we replicate that in our community? This introduction will help you answer those questions. First, it will outline some success factors—keys to ensuring a positive and productive assessment experience. It will also describe a variety of possible goals and strategies that drive design choices when selecting an approach to organizational assessment. Finally, the introduction will explore in more depth some of the design choices you will face when planning an assessment effort.

The best approach to organizational assessment for your organization and your community is one that is uniquely tailored to fit your goals, resources, needs, and constraints.

The best approach to organizational assessment for your organization and your community is one that is uniquely tailored to fit your goals, resources, needs, and constraints. Use the examples in this book to tweak your imagination and give you ideas, and then use your best strategic thinking skills. Along with a little help from your nonprofit allies, you can create a successful assessment program, whether your goal is to build capacity in nonprofits, enhance your grantmaking, impact systems, or strengthen the nonprofit sector.

Success Factors

Many factors need to be carefully considered to conduct or sponsor either a successful organizational assessment or a broader assessment program. Some factors will be covered at the end of the introduction in the section called Design Choices. Six success factors deserve special mention:

- Depth and breadth of skill needed

- Commitment and buy-in

- A well-tested framework

- Accurate and complete information

- Confidentiality and ownership of findings

- Clear expectations regarding use of findings

These factors have implications for the approach you choose and the resources you will need to do assessment well. Although success factors for grantmaker and grantee assessment will be similar, this chapter will focus primarily on grantee assessment because it tends to involve a more delicate relationship.

Depth and breadth of skill needed

Using sensitive, impartial, experienced, and skilled people to conduct the assessment (referred to here as *consultants* or *the assessment team*[1]) is critical to getting the best results. Consultants should possess organizational expertise, industry knowledge, and process skills. Ideally an assessment team will have at least two members to allow for a broader range of expertise and to ensure that issues aren't missed. Team members with a high degree of organization development experience and industry knowledge not only will be better able to identify issues during the assessment, but also will have greater credibility with the organization. This credibility improves the relationship with, and in-depth probing of, organizational stakeholders. It also increases the depth of the

---

[1] It is possible for one person to conduct an effective assessment if that person has the skills and experience needed. If using a team approach, usually at least one person is from outside the organization. Internal people can be on the team to help plan the process, gather information, help with logistics, and ensure good communication takes place.

analysis of organizational strengths and challenges. If the nonprofit believes that the consultants are highly qualified and bring new competencies and expert knowledge to the process, the consultants are almost assured of collecting important information needed for a successful assessment.

Commitment and buy-in

Readiness and openness to learning on the part of the nonprofit is critical; the organization should be able to identify how it will gain from the experience at the beginning. For this reason it is more effective if the assessment is proposed by the organization, or at least is viewed as being done *with* them, rather than *to* them. Buy-in from both board and staff will maximize the chance that the organization will heed assessment findings and implement needed changes. If the executive director is the only nonprofit representative deeply involved in the assessment, then the findings will "belong" to that executive director. The risk is that if the executive director resigns, the remaining staff and board will have no ownership in the assessment, and its utility will be short-lived. Involving key board members and staff from the outset—from selecting the assessment method and consultant to participating in strategy discussions—helps them to become deeply committed to the process and mitigates this risk. Some assessments will include two to three staff or board members on the assessment team with the consultants to help plan the process and ensure clear communications. Broad participation and commitment also benefit the funder; it ensures that a full range of issues is considered and minimizes potential problems and resistance to change.

A well-tested framework

A well-tested assessment framework and assessment tools will ensure that critical issues aren't missed and that there is a theoretical or researched basis for the analysis and recommendations. A variety of frameworks can be purchased, used with permission, or adapted to fit particular needs. The assessment programs profiled in this book offer some useful, well-tested examples.

A framework for organization effectiveness should describe what components are viewed as critical to the organization's functioning, and how these components interact and perform in a well-functioning organization. Different models or frameworks appear in the literature because people place greater or lesser weight on individual components, use different terminology, or have tailored their model to a particular kind of organization. After thoroughly studying the literature, we've landed on the model described in Figure 1, Components of Organizational Capacity, page 6. Each of the components described in this model have specific indicators that describe the organization's current level of functioning. Note that each of the seven components contains many aspects of organizational operations that can be assessed alone or in combination with others. For example, you can conduct a thorough assessment of an organization's financial position and working capital, as Nonprofit Finance Fund (NFF) does.[2] NFF's Nonprofit Business Analysis assesses the finances, programs, and business models of nonprofit organizations, and evaluates their readiness for change, including moving, renovating space, growing, downsizing, or receiving a grant or loan.

When reviewing possible frameworks to use, make sure that the particular issues you want to address are included in the framework. Consider using a combination of tools if the issues you want to focus on aren't available in one source. For example, you may want to look at broad aspects of organization effectiveness and do an in-depth assessment of the organization's program impact. In that case, consider using two tools, or combining an organizational assessment with a program review. Another example comes from this book. In looking at foundation effectiveness, the SMART GROWTH tools provide an overall assessment of twelve aspects of organizational effectiveness, while the Grantee Perception Report considers feedback from a foundation's grantees. Used together these tools would provide rich feedback and a blueprint for action.

Consider using a combination of tools if the issues you want to focus on aren't available in one source.

If you are choosing consultant(s) to conduct assessments, be sure to talk through with them the various models and frameworks they typically use. If you need multiple consultants to work with a framework you have selected, make sure that the consultants have a common understanding of industry standards—what constitutes outstanding, acceptable, or inadequate performance in each area or indicator. Also, ensure that they are able to clearly and confidently communicate this framework to the nonprofits they work with.

---

[2] http://www.nonprofitfinancefund.org

Figure 1. Components of Organizational Capacity [3]

Capacity is an abstract term that describes a wide range of capabilities, knowledge, and resources that nonprofits need in order to be effective. What makes an organization effective? According to Grantmakers for Effective Organizations, it is "an organization's ability to fulfill its mission measurably through a blend of sound management, strong governance, and a persistent rededication to assessing and achieving results."[4] Organizational capacity is multifaceted and continually evolving. Six components of organizational capacity are necessary for high performance: governance and leadership; mission, vision, and strategy; program delivery and impact; strategic relationships; resource development; and internal operations and management. These interdependent factors all contribute to the health and performance of a nonprofit organization.

Governance and Leadership: The organization's board of directors is engaged and representative, with defined governance practices. The board effectively oversees the policies, programs, and organizational operations including reviewing achievement of strategic goals, financial status, and executive director performance. The organization is accomplished at recruiting, developing, and retaining capable staff and technical resources. The organization's leadership is alert to changing community needs and realities.

Mission, Vision, and Strategy: The organization has a vital mission and a clear understanding of its identity. It is actively involved in regular, results-oriented, strategic, and self-reflective thinking and planning that aligns strategies with the mission and organizational capacity. The planning process involves stakeholders in an ongoing dialogue that ensures that the organization's mission and programs are valuable to the neighborhood or constituency it serves.

Program Delivery and Impact: The organization operates programs that demonstrate tangible outcomes commensurate with the resources invested. Programs are high quality and well regarded. The organization utilizes program evaluation results to inform its strategic goals. The organization has formal mechanisms for assessing internal and external factors that affect achievement of goals.

Strategic Relationships: The organization is a respected and active participant and leader in the community, and maintains strong connections with its constituents. It participates in strategic alliances and partnerships that significantly advance its goals and expand influence.

Resource Development: The organization successfully secures support from a variety of sources to ensure that its revenues are diversified, stable, and sufficient for the mission and goals. The resource development plan is aligned with the mission, long-term goals, and strategic direction. The organization has high visibility with key stakeholders, and links clear, strategic messages to its resource development efforts.

Internal Operations and Management: The organization has efficient and effective operations, and strong management support systems. Financial operations are responsibly managed and reflect sound accounting principles. The organization utilizes information effectively for organizational and project management purposes. Asset, risk, and technology management are strong and appropriate to the organization's purpose.[5]

Mission, vision, and strategy are the driving forces that give the organization its purpose and direction. Program delivery and impact are the nonprofit's primary reasons for existence, just as profit is a primary aim for many for-profit companies.

---

[3] Excerpt from Paul Connolly and Carol Lukas, *Strengthening Nonprofit Performance: A Funder's Guide to Capacity Building* (Saint Paul, MN: Fieldstone Alliance, 2002). Available from Fieldstone Alliance at http://www.FieldstoneAlliance.org

[4] http://www.geofunders.org

Strategic relationships, resource development, and internal operations and management are all necessary mechanisms to achieve the organization's ends. Absent any one of them, an organization flounders or does not reach its full potential. Leadership and governance is the lubricant that keeps all the parts aligned and moving. The model also suggests the need for constant feedback from the external environment, and routine monitoring of program audience and outcomes to inform mission and strategy. When assessing nonprofits and planning intervention strategies it is best to examine each element separately, in relation to the others, and within the organization's overall context.

A variety of factors can influence an organization's needs at any time, including

- Age and developmental stage of the organization
- Size of the organization
- Kind of work the organization does
- Cultural or ethnic identity of the organization
- Environment in which the organization functions

Components of Organizational Capacity

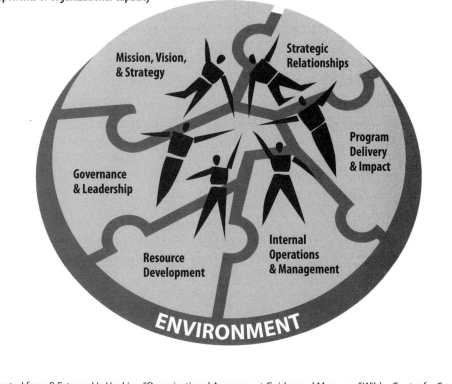

---

5   Adapted from P. Fate and L. Hoskins, "Organizational Assessment Guides and Measures," Wilder Center for Communities (2001). Some of these components are derived from N. Glickman, and L. Servon, "More than Bricks and Sticks: Five Components of Community Development Corporations' Capacity," *Housing Policy Debate* 9 (1998) 497–539.

Accurate and complete information

Getting accurate and complete information is both a challenge and a necessity. It is human nature to resist disclosing personal or sensitive information to people who don't inspire your trust and confidence. Building trust requires time and a skillful assessment team. Steps to ensure that accurate information is collected include

- Selecting consultants who inspire confidence and assure impartiality throughout the process

- Ensuring that the board and staff are deeply committed to the assessment process and that they encourage everyone to provide honest, thoughtful information

- Gathering information from multiple sources: board, staff, volunteers, and external stakeholders

- Being transparent about what information will be shared, with whom it will be shared, and how the findings will be used

Confidentiality and ownership of findings

Nonprofits typically are eager to learn the assessment findings, but fearful of others having access to the same findings. Will they be judged, compared to other nonprofits, and suffer in the comparison? The key to avoiding these concerns is clarifying up front who owns the information, how it will be shared, and how it will be used.

The nonprofit's and funder's agreement on information ownership and access should be disclosed at the outset of the process and at the beginning of each interview. Assessment findings should be shared with the executive director before they are included in the final report. Giving the director an opportunity to review, dispute, and potentially amend any findings before publication eliminates the fear of unpleasant surprises. The final report is generally shared with key staff and the board, although who sees the report and how it is used will vary based on the goals and strategies used. Some hold that a funder should never see the assessment report; in other cases, where the funder commissions the assessment, they may see an executive summary of findings and recommendations. If the nonprofit that is being assessed knows that the funder will see the entire report, parties are less likely to divulge accurate information and perceptions. Whether or not the funder sees the complete assessment report or a summary of key findings and recommendations should be negotiated *prior* to beginning the assessment.

Clear expectations regarding use of findings

Nonprofits have concerns at the beginning of an assessment such as, Will the assessment findings affect our funding? Could we risk losing our funding altogether? Will we be forced to implement all of the recommendations or will we have choices about how we respond to the findings?

How the funder will use the assessment findings should be clear at the beginning of the process. If nonprofits see only risk in the undertaking, they are unlikely to participate willingly, or to share complete information. For assessment to have the greatest impact, it is critical that the process be designed as a journey of learning and discovery rather than as a test or judgment. The rest of the introduction will outline choices to help maximize the learning process.

> **For assessment to have the greatest impact it is critical that the process be designed as a journey of learning and discovery rather than as a test or judgment.**

If the funder and the nonprofit agree on the implications of the findings and the expectations each has for implementation, the path to a successful assessment will be clear. Assessment is most appropriately used as a critical step in a development process—or as a journey of discovery and learning—rather than as a means of deciding whether or not to pull funding. Some funders only assess organizations after they make it through the due diligence process and receive a grant award. For example, once an initial grant is awarded, Social Venture Partners of Seattle (SVP) asks grantees (whom it terms "investees") to complete a capacity assessment tool to help assess their organizational capacity and establish goals and benchmarks so progress in building capacity can be measured over time.[6] More information on SVP Seattle's capacity assessment process is available in Chapter 1.

---

[6] http://www.svpseattle.org/about_svp/model.htm

These six success factors need careful consideration and attention when planning and implementing an assessment program. Anytime an outsider enters an organization, he or she disturbs the life of the group, no matter how well-intentioned the outsider is. An assessment is this kind of disturbance. Done poorly or insensitively, it can cause conflict, frustration, loss of productivity, and resentment within the organization. Done well, it can launch the organization to a new and stronger stage in its development.

To craft an effective assessment program, or even support one assessment, it is helpful to clarify what you hope to achieve, and to explore a range of possible strategies for reaching your goal. The following section explores four goals and gives examples of strategies that can achieve those goals.

Assessment Goals and the Strategies to Achieve Them

We all know that form follows function, and that it is usually wisest to be clear about our goals before deciding on a particular strategy. Yet it is all too easy to passionately debate the pros and cons of various assessment approaches without considering what you hope to achieve. Because organizational assessment can be done in so many different ways, and affect so many levels, take the time to explore a range of possible goals and strategies.

If you as a grantmaker are considering investing in organizational assessments, you are most likely trying to achieve one of five goals:

1. Build the capacity of nonprofits
2. Enhance grantmaking
3. Impact systems
4. Strengthen the nonprofit sector
5. Measure your own effectiveness

The following pages discuss each of these goals along with some typical strategies grantmakers use to accomplish them.

Goal 1. Build the capacity of nonprofits

Nonprofit organizations can most effectively develop a strategic plan, create new programs, downsize their operations, or expand their service area if they have a clear and accurate picture of themselves and their environment. An assessment provides that picture by analyzing many factors—the nonprofits' mission, values, strategies, performance over time, strengths and capabilities, external needs, partnerships, resources, and opportunities for achieving greater impact in the future. Using the assessment's findings, nonprofits can successfully determine the strategies needed to improve performance. Here are five strategies grantmakers can use to help nonprofits build their capacity:

- Provide grants for assessment directly to nonprofits
- Fund capacity-building providers to conduct assessments
- Form a consultant pool
- Monitor nonprofit performance over time
- Link the assessment with other change processes

Provide grants for assessment directly to nonprofits

Using this strategy, funders make grants to the nonprofits; the organizations then select the assessment approach and the consultant and guide the process. The benefit of this strategy is that it ensures the organizations' commitment to the assessment process allows them to select the approach and consultant that fits with their organizational culture, and offers the opportunity to adapt the process to meet their needs. While this strategy reduces the amount of time that funders must commit to guiding the process, it also reduces their role in ensuring a minimal level of quality and impartiality. Some nonprofits do not like this strategy for the same reasons. The nonprofits carry the burden of determining who will conduct the assessment and the responsibility of crafting the assessment design.

Fund capacity-building providers to conduct assessments

Some grantmakers subsidize or cover the cost of assessments by making grants to nonprofit consulting groups (management support organizations) or by contracting with consultants to conduct assessments. They might also screen consultants to ensure that those funded have an adequate level of expertise to conduct the assessments. Grantmakers identify their goals and expectations, and rely on the providers to appropriately customize the assessment to meet those goals. A benefit of this approach is that the providers (not the time-strapped funders) assume responsibility for problems that may arise. A challenge posed by this approach relates to ownership of information. If the providers are "hired" by the funders, to whom do they report? *It is critical that the nonprofits own the findings* and that the nonprofits, rather than the providers, report the results to the funders.

Form a consultant pool

Several benefits can result from forming a pool of consultants skilled in assessment from which nonprofits can then select. Consultants with organizational expertise and industry knowledge can be invited to join the pool. Grantmakers can establish overall standards and expectations, train the consultants, and select the framework to be used in the assessments, yet nonprofits can select the consultant of their choice—offering each a measure of control at the outset. This strategy offers the additional benefit of elasticity—a large number of nonprofits to be assessed can be managed relatively simply with an equally large consultant pool. Hartford Foundation for Public Giving, in its Nonprofit Support Program (NSP), contracts with a small pool of consultants who are carefully screened and trained to conduct assessments. When a nonprofit requests an assessment, NSP selects the consultant, and then the consultant works directly with the nonprofit to tailor the process and schedule to suit the nonprofit's needs. NSP uses the same assessment framework for all nonprofits going through the assessment process.

Monitor nonprofit performance over time

Measuring and evaluating nonprofit performance over time is a useful strategy when funders want a long view of specific variables. Analyzing performance over time yields some insights into the effect that changes—demographic, operational, strategic, or programmatic—have on outcomes. This methodology contrasts with a one-time assessment that provides a single deep look at a nonprofit. Assessments focused on measuring performance over a longer time period generally use, at least in part, a quantitative data collection approach. The same instrument(s) can then be administered at intervals to determine changes over time. The Pew Charitable Trusts' Philadelphia Cultural Leadership Program (PCLP) uses assessment as an entry to their three-year operating support funding program. Organizations receiving funding may reapply for the program three years later, which involves going through another assessment. Some organizations are now on their third round of funding in PCLP, allowing Pew to see changes not only in individual organizations, but also in the field of arts and culture organizations that they fund.

Link the assessment with other change processes

Linking the assessment with other change processes can increase its impact. Most often it is linked with a strategic planning process, providing the critical foundation to the strategic planning discussions that follow. The assessment can also be a valuable lead-in to planning a significant expansion of the organization, a major programmatic redirection, or even an anticipated merger.

Goal 2. Enhance grantmaking

Organizational assessment can enhance the quality and impact of your grantmaking in several ways. It does not have to be a distinct program to get results. It can be the first step in a series of funding awards to help an organization develop over time. It can be incorporated into other program-related grants that you make and strengthened by increasing your program officers' skill at organizational review. If you are interested in strengthening your own grantmaking organization, you might consider starting with an assessment as well, which can lead to enhanced grantmaking and in turn greater capacity in nonprofits. Four approaches will help with this goal:

- Make sequential grants
- Train program officers in first-level assessment
- Incorporate assessment into program or project grants
- Conduct an assessment of your own organization

Make sequential grants

Nonprofits frequently approach funders asking for a capacity-building grant to "strengthen our fundraising," or "improve marketing efforts," or "hold a board retreat." Savvy grantmakers will question whether those efforts are really what the organizations most need, and may even have some evidence that other more systemic factors affect the organizations' success. Rather than turning down the request or arguing about what they really need, you might suggest that you would support the cost of an organizational assessment to get a handle on the organization's range and priority of needs. In the end, you may end up providing the funds for the fundraising or board retreat, but at least you will know with certainty that future capacity-building investments in that organization are grounded in an objective view of their needs and potential. Making grants sequentially for a series of change processes can be a powerful incentive for nonprofits to engage in each process completely, so as to ensure the next process will also be funded.

Train program officers in first-level assessment

Most grantmakers perform due diligence before making any grant. This process, whether informal and intuitive or formal and structured, is a form of assessment. This first-level assessment is more superficial than an in-depth assessment but can be effective in uncovering both strengths and possible areas for improvement in the organization. However, even first-level assessments require skills and sensitivity that aren't necessarily gained through experience working in a nonprofit, foundation, or in a variety of other professions. Training in how to review and analyze organizational dynamics and functioning can greatly enhance the quality of this initial assessment.

Incorporate assessment into program or project grants

In their passion to reach more people and get better results, nonprofits often start up or expand programs without considering the impact the new or expanded program will have on the rest of the organization. To combat this issue, consider building an assessment into other grants for project or program development. In this case, an assessment serves both the funder and the nonprofit by encouraging a deep look at the organization and its environment before launching a major new initiative, and ensuring that the organization has the capacity to sustain the new program over time.

Conduct an assessment of your own organization

Whether new or established, expanding or downsizing, with a stable focus or changing focus, an assessment can give your grantmaking organization the same objective picture it provides for the nonprofits you support. An assessment can help inform strategic choices that you are making, tell you how to strengthen your community visibility or relationships, or address how to improve donor relations. The added bonus is that going through an assessment will help you understand the process that your grantees go through and will demonstrate to them, loud and clear, that you "walk your talk." What feels the most risky, yet has the greatest potential for payoff, is to involve your grantees in the assessment as informants, and to share at least some of the findings with them. This demonstration of transparency will earn you great esteem in the community. The second part of this book highlights two tools grantmakers can use for self-assessment: The Grantee Perception Survey, from the Center for Effective Philanthropy, and the SMART GROWTH Assessment Tool, developed by Women's Funding Network.

Goal 3. Impact systems

Increasingly, grantmakers are using organizational assessments to determine how best to impact nonprofits working in a specific field, geographic area, or population. Conducting a series of assessments for related organizations offers the opportunity to identify patterns and common issues that can be addressed *across the field* of organizations, rather than just one by one. In addition, this data can be useful to organizations and grantmakers in other communities. Two approaches will help you achieve the goal of impacting broad systems:

- Assess organizations in clusters or systems
- Use assessment as a screening tool

Assess organizations in clusters or systems

Clustered assessments, those conducted for a group of related organizations, provide information that can be applied not only to the assessed organizations, but also to related organizations. For organizations serving a similar mission but spread over a wide geographic area, a series of assessments can identify common success factors, lead to peer learning and shared successful strategies, and highlight opportunities for collaborative action or even strategic restructuring of the organizations. When different organizations serve the same population or geographic area, assessments can help the groups consider collaborative ways to address challenges they are facing. When groups of related organizations are assessed, a coordinated assessment package, with consistent processes and frameworks, can be developed and distributed to those who will be conducting the assessments. This serves two purposes: first, the package incorporates material unique to the field or community, and second, findings can be aggregated to bring to the surface common themes, trends, and development needs.

> **When different organizations serve the same population or geographic area, assessments can help the groups consider collaborative ways to address challenges they are facing.**

For example, the Department of Housing and Urban Development funded Habitat for Humanity International to assess a group of five urban affiliates to determine the factors that most contributed to their success—with the hope that this information would strengthen performance among all urban affiliates in the United States. After the success factors were identified, case studies and tools for each success factor were developed and have become the backbone of a knowledge-sharing system across all Habitat urban affiliates. Another example is the Community Clinics Initiative (CCI), a joint project of Tides Foundation and the California Endowment. The project's mission is to help increase the organizational capacity of individual clinics in California and build the capacity of the field. CCI used a customized version of McKinsey's Capacity Assessment Grid to gather data to create a portrait of organizational capacity across all community clinics and health centers in California. CCI is using this portrait to stimulate dialogue among clinics, infrastructure organizations, and grantmakers about the field's capacity needs and ways to address them.

Use assessment as a screening tool

There's a wide range of opinion and practice regarding using assessments as a screening tool. Some funders require assessment prior to a funding decision. For example, the Unity Foundation in Maine requires an assessment (see Chapter 4) before applying for a capacity-building grant. Prior to chartering an organization, Neighborhood Reinvestment Corporation conducts an assessment to evaluate whether basic systems are in place and whether the nonprofit has sufficient community and financial support to ensure ongoing success. However, other funders believe strongly in not using assessments in this manner for a variety of reasons. When used as a screening tool, assessment can be viewed as a hoop to jump through rather than a developmental process, and the likelihood of getting inaccurate information increases.

Goal 4. Strengthen the nonprofit sector

Many funders hope that, in addition to building capacity within individual nonprofits, they can strengthen the nonprofit sector locally or nationally. To do this, field-building strategies need to be considered, such as investing in improving the assessment skills of consultants; expanding the number of consultants trained in organizational assessment; or conducting, packaging, and disseminating research, promising practices, and industry-specific data related to organizational performance. Two approaches will help a grantmaker achieve this goal:

- Train consultants to do effective assessments
- Conduct and disseminate research based on assessment results

Train consultants to do effective assessment

Enhancing the skills of capacity builders is a powerful strategy that can benefit many nonprofits for years to come. Organizational assessment requires a complex mix of skills and knowledge and, to be done well, requires an experienced person or a team of people with complementary skill sets. Many communities lack people trained in this level of data gathering and analysis, with knowledge of organizational theory and models, with industry knowledge, and with the intervention and process skills to create a positive experience of discovery. Funders can strengthen the nonprofit sector by sponsoring training that will enlarge the pool and deepen the skills of consultants in conducting assessments. Most grantmakers don't have the skills required to conduct this training themselves. Trainers can be found through national intermediaries, management support organizations, experienced consultants, and academic institutions.

Conduct and disseminate research based on assessment results

Assessment findings, analyzed across a broad array of organizations, can provide performance benchmarks for other organizations, highlight trends in the sector, or uncover clues to leadership challenges for boards and executives. Funders across the country are constantly looking for *what works,* and how to *increase impact.* If we can begin to uncover patterns, such as the discouragingly low percentage of organizations that have a succession plan for their executive, or the high turnover rate of entry-level nonprofit workers, we have a chance of heading off future crises in the sector.

These four goals—build the capacity of nonprofits, enhance grantmaking, impact systems, and strengthen the nonprofit sector—are the most common goals that drive assessments. Other goals may motivate you to respond to critical community needs to gain greater visibility, or to partner with other funders. Whatever the motivation is, organizational assessment can be a highly effective way of helping nonprofits increase their performance, scale, reach, and impact.

Goal 5. Measure your own effectiveness

Grantmakers concerned about the effectiveness of their grantees should pay equal attention to the capacity of their own organizations. Part 2 of this book, Assessing Funder Capacity, describes two capacity assessment tools available for grantmakers. As a grantmaker, conducting a capacity assessment process of your own organization gives you firsthand knowledge of the reservations grantees might have when asked to participate in an assessment. It can be difficult to admit weaknesses, much less show them to someone else. Grantmakers can have a positive influence on grantees by being as open and honest about their own challenges as they expect grantees to be with theirs. Chapter 5, Turning the Tables on Assessment: The Grantee Perception Report, provides examples of grantmakers who have shared the results of their Grantee Perception

Report—warts and all—with grantees and the public as an effort to demonstrate accountability and commitment to improving their own effectiveness.

Design Choices

Once you've clarified your goals and selected broad strategies to use, you need to sort through the details of how to implement the assessment. The assessment programs described in this book contain numerous variations that give each program its unique character and emphasis. Each of these programs evolved into its final form through a design process—a sorting out of choices. As you sort through the choices, here are some of the questions that must be answered.

- Should we sponsor self-assessments or hire consultants to do them?
- Does our community have enough skilled consultants?
- How many organizations do we expect to put through the program each year? If we can only afford two or three, will we be inundated with demand we can't address?
- Will the same process and instrument work for a variety of organizations, even if they work in different fields?
- How much latitude can we give nonprofits to change the assessment to suit their needs?
- We could do more if we partner with other funders, but how much work would that be? Could we ever come to agreement?

Your design decisions need to align your strategy and approach with the goals you are trying to achieve. Five of the most critical design choices are explored below:

- Deciding depth and scale
- Self-assessment versus third-party assessment
- Quantitative or qualitative approach
- Degree of customization
- Going it alone or collaborating with other funders

Deciding depth and scale

Many of the assessment strategies described in this chapter require deep assessments of a few organizations. A *deep assessment* involves customized techniques such as extensive one-on-one interviews with key internal and external stakeholders and research of environmental or industry data. Deep assessments are useful when the assessment is a prelude to a larger effort, such as significant funding, expansion of services, or organizational restructuring. In these cases, the investment in extensive fact-finding and analysis is justified by the scope of the work to follow. While critical to the success of the subsequent work, these assessments are also expensive and time-intensive, and may limit the resources that are available to other organizations. A deep assessment of a few organizations is effective in achieving the goals of *building nonprofit capacity* and *enhancing grantmaking,* by linking the assessment with other change processes or future program or capacity grants.

Other strategies may suggest a broad-brush assessment of multiple organizations. A *broad-brush assessment* lacks the intensive analysis characteristic of a deep assessment. Rather, it examines a fixed number of critical indicators within many organizations. In essence, it provides a snapshot view of each organization, using standardized assessment tools that can be administered and compiled fairly simply. This approach may be more useful if the goal is to *strengthen the nonprofit sector* through conducting and disseminating research based on assessment results. With a broad-brush assessment, it may be possible to include a much larger pool of organizations and thereby get more reliable data. A broad-brush assessment can also focus on a vertical view of a few selected challenges unique to the organizations, such as advocacy practices, development partnerships, or earned income performance. The vertical view using a broad-brush assessment may be appropriate when the goal is *impacting systems* by assessing organizations in clusters or fields.

Self-assessment versus third-party assessment

When flexible timing, a lower cost, and more general insights are called for, then a self-assessment can be the appropriate design. Self-assessments typically use survey instruments and compile the perceptions of selected staff, board members, and often outside stakeholders. The organization, the funder, or an impartial third-party can compile the results. Self-assessments, if administered to a broad enough sample of organizations, can measure an organization against industry standards. For the nonprofit, self-assessments entail less risk of exposing potentially embarrassing issues to their funder, and are less disruptive to the organization's day-to-day work schedules. Getting buy-in from the staff and board is fairly simple. It is also a process that the nonprofit may opt to repeat themselves, at intervals suited to their own needs. What self-assessments lack is the impartial third-party view. While a self-assessment does signal that it is time to step back and consider how effective the nonprofit has been, it is somewhat like the choir preaching to themselves—no new voices are heard. With no outside input it is difficult for an organization to objectively measure many aspects of their organization; it is especially difficult to measure their leadership, strategies, and quality of service—three of the most critical variables in organizational functioning. However, self-assessments can be an effective design when the goal is to monitor certain aspects of nonprofit performance over time, or to collect concrete data from a large field of organizations.

A third party adds immeasurably to the quality and depth of the assessment findings. A trained consultant can ask questions of stakeholders that nonprofit staff would be uncomfortable asking. A third party is there to do one thing—conduct the assessment—and is not hindered by concern for how individual perceptions might harm working relationships with board members, clients, nonprofit partners, or funders. In addition, a third party brings their own field expertise and organizational knowledge to the process. They can see connections between issues, analyze how the organizational strategy, systems, and culture may or may not be supporting the mission, and frame the feedback to the organization in a helpful way that elevates the discussion of future direction. These important benefits of a third-party assessment are offset by some challenges, including the greater expense, the difficulty of finding a skilled consultant, and the risk that the consultant won't deliver high-quality work.

Funders should not conduct an assessment beyond the due diligence or first-level review for several reasons. First, funders are unlikely to get complete and accurate information. Second, few funders have sufficient knowledge, skill, and experience to do an in-depth assessment covering all aspects of the organization's functioning. And third, funders are not impartial and run the risk of either inflating or diminishing the organization's strengths and challenges. If there are no other choices, it is important to build some kind of firewall to provide confidentiality and impartiality to the organization and ensure that funding decisions are sound.

Quantitative or qualitative approach

Most assessment findings contain a mix of quantitative and qualitative data. Different skill sets are needed by those who conduct assessments using the two approaches. Collecting objective, quantitative data is more straightforward and less arguable; it can be objectively evaluated and compared across systems and communities. Assessments using quantitative tools lend themselves well to benchmarking, and to the development of key indicators of success. Assessments that are primarily quantitative are a good design choice for *building nonprofit capacity* by measuring nonprofit performance over time. They are also effective when *strengthening the nonprofit sector* by conducting and disseminating research.

But quantitative tools tell only part of the story. They illustrate trends and cast some light on current issues, but not enough light to develop complete recommendations as part of the assessment. And they do a poor job of considering the effect of leadership, mission, strategy, culture, and partnerships on the organization. To get a complete picture of how an organization is functioning it is necessary to look at how parts of the system interact, and the effectiveness of leadership in keeping the parts working together. Those who conduct qualitative assessments must be expert at distilling and analyzing subjective data—organizational perceptions, stakeholders' insights, and their own skilled observations—to develop useful conclusions and recommendations. An assessment that combines quantitative and qualitative methods will provide the most complete and accurate picture of the organization's functioning.

Degree of customization

Numerous research reports and publications on capacity-building success factors[7] highlight customization—one size does not fit all—as a critical factor in the success of a development effort. Organizations vary by age, stage, culture,

---

[7] For two such studies see Connolly and Lukas, *Strengthening Nonprofit Performance.*

size, field, and environmental factors. To be most effective, the assessment process, focus, instruments, consultant's style and experience, timing, and reporting need to be tailored to suit the particular needs of each organization.

There are many advantages to customizing assessments. Customizing assessment tools, or the overall process itself, allows for a sharper focus on issues of greatest salience to the nonprofit and interest to the funder. For example, the funder may want to know how adding supportive family services affects the number of families a community development corporation can house in low-cost rental units. Or a funder may want to measure how operating under a strategic plan affects nonprofit productivity. One nonprofit may have particular interest in learning whether residents in their neighborhood feel that the organization is accessible. Another nonprofit may have had recent board turnover and be more interested in the new board's perceptions of the organization. Forcing these nonprofits into a fixed framework may not meet their needs.

The disadvantages of customization include greater cost, increased difficulty comparing results across groups of nonprofits, and difficulty finding consultants with experience in a broad and flexible range of research methods.

At times, using an off-the-shelf assessment instrument is sufficient. Using tested tools eliminates the risk of a poorly designed, untested set of tools derailing the assessment process. A tested tool can be put into use quickly, and reduces the development time needed before beginning the actual assessment. It also produces more standardized data when used by multiple consultants, reducing the likelihood of different interpretations of organizational conditions. The standardized assessment may have a limited scope, but that limitation can be outweighed by the lower cost and ease of delivery.

A hybrid approach can be effective—using standardized instruments and adapting the process to suit each organization's preferences. The consultants first learn the standard tools and processes needed to conduct assessments. They are then positioned to customize—either a little or a lot—for the next organization as needed.

Going it alone or collaborating with other funders

Funders plan and implement assessment programs on their own for many reasons. Working alone is easier, less time consuming, and eliminates the need to negotiate or compromise on goals, strategies, or design elements. Working alone, the funder will get all the visibility and goodwill that may accrue from their investment. However, in some cases, working alone may limit the number of organizations you can impact or the depth of the assessments you are able to conduct. In a collaborative effort with other funders or intermediaries, there is the possibility of multiplying your investment and impact.

When a more comprehensive assessment program is called for, collaboration among funders can be very effective. If a large number of nonprofits are to be assessed, one funder may need to combine resources with another. Assessments may require multiple areas of expertise, such as a combination of organizational development and industry expertise. For example, assessing a group of community development corporations may demand deep knowledge of leadership development and nonprofit structure, paired with specific experience with real estate development partnerships or financing mechanisms. Increasingly funders are training their sights on community impact. When assessment is intended to build the capacity of organizations to impact broader systems or communities, you may need more expertise and connections at the table when planning the assessments. Collaborating with other funders may also be appropriate when the organization intends to seek funding from multiple sources at the completion of the assessment.

There is no right answer to these design choices, nor a perfect way to provide assessments to your constituents. Each grantmaking organization needs to weave through the tangle of possibilities and find the approach that best suits both your mission and goals and the organizations and communities you serve. The cases in this book illustrate many different successful assessment designs to consider. They offer a creative "kick-start" to help identify and fine-tune your own approach—one that will help you and the nonprofits you support achieve your goals.

Summary

Just as many of us become "house blind," failing to see the stacks of clutter and dust bunnies under the couch, so too do many organizations get used to how they operate. They may no longer realize that they are spinning their wheels, have ineffective systems, or even that they have tremendous untapped capabilities to improve their performance. Assessment can deliver many kinds of results. It can increase organizations' efficiencies, multiply impact, reinvigorate sleeping boards, and spur them in new directions. Assessment can help funders build the capacity of nonprofits, enhance grantmaking, impact systems, or strengthen the nonprofit sector. Assessment truly is a powerful change strategy. Like all forms of power, it must be handled with care—and used wisely.

PART ONE

Grantee Assessment Tools

Using a capacity assessment tool can be a constructive way for a grantmaker and grantee to work together to identify grantee capacity challenges and priority areas for funding. However, the types of tools available, the goals of grantmakers who use them, and the way in which they are administered are as diverse as the philanthropic sector itself. This section shares grantmakers' stories in using four different tools to assess grantee capacity.

CHAPTER 1

Building Capacity While Assessing It

Three Foundations' Experiences Using the McKinsey Capacity Assessment Grid

by Kendall Guthrie and Alan Preston, Blueprint Research & Design, Inc.,[8] *with assistance from Erin Hemmings, Social Venture Partners Seattle; Chantel L. Walker and Sarita Siqueiros, the Marguerite Casey Foundation; and Ellen Friedman and Kathy Lim Ko, The Community Clinics Initiative*

Successful organizational capacity assessment efforts strike a delicate balance between gathering information useful to funders and helping grantees better understand their own capacity. This chapter highlights the work of three innovative grantmakers that achieved that equilibrium by building a capacity assessment process around a tailored version of the McKinsey Capacity Assessment Grid.[9] Social Venture Partners (SVP) Seattle, the Marguerite Casey Foundation, and the Community Clinics Initiative (CCI, a joint project of the Tides Foundation and the California Endowment) each used a customized version of this self-assessment tool. The process helped grantees better understand strengths and weaknesses in their own organizational capacity and also provided the funders valuable data to inform their overall program planning.

---

[8] The authors would like to give special thanks to other members of the Blueprint staff: Stephanie Fuerstner Gillis, Amy Luckey, Justin Louie, and Cory Sbarbaro. Each of these people worked on one or more of the capacity assessment projects described in this research and contributed many ideas to this article.

[9] The Capacity Assessment Grid was created by McKinsey & Company for Venture Philanthropy Partners (http://www.vppartners.org) and published in *Effective Capacity Building in Nonprofit Organizations* (Reston, VA: Venture Philanthropy Partners, 2001).

While the three funders had somewhat different goals for the assessment process, they all sought a design that emphasized helping grantees rather than judging them. Together, through a process that successfully stimulated both grantee and foundation-wide learning, these three foundations have used this approach with more than two hundred grantees, ranging from small advocacy organizations to multimillion-dollar service providers.

Blueprint Research & Design, Inc. (Blueprint), a strategy and evaluation consulting firm for philanthropic organizations, first helped each funder to identify its goals for capacity assessment. Blueprint then worked with each grantmaker to customize the grid to meet those respective goals and fit their mission. The customization process generally included gathering feedback from grantees who pilot tested the original McKinsey Grid, developing new questions to address the foundations' unique interests, reorganizing aspects of the instrument, pilot testing the revised version, administering the survey to all grantees, and analyzing the data to look at patterns in organizational capacity across grantees. A cross section of grantees was interviewed about its experiences using the instrument. At the end of this process, Blueprint provided

Chapter Overview

This chapter shares the stories of three grantmakers who adapted the McKinsey Grid, a framework for conceptualizing different components of organizational capacity that includes a self-assessment tool to help nonprofits identify their capacity strengths and weaknesses. The text covers the following topics:

- Reasons for foundations to conduct a capacity assessment
- Lessons on successful implementation
- Lessons about interpreting assessment data
- Recommendations for customizing the McKinsey Grid

In-depth information about Social Venture Partners Seattle, the Marguerite Casey Foundation, and the Community Clinics Initiative, their capacity-building goals, and use of the McKinsey Grid can be found at the end of this chapter.

The CD-ROM that accompanies this book includes the following materials to support this chapter:

- *McKinsey Capacity Assessment Grid*
- *Report to the Field: Assessing the Capacity of California's Community Clinics: A Report on the Community Clinics Initiative's 2003 Building Capacities Self-Assessment Survey*
- *CCI Building Capacities Self-Assessment Tool*
- *Marguerite Casey Foundation Organizational Capacity Assessment Tool*
- *SVP Organizational Capacity Assessment Tool*

each grantmaker with recommendations for using the assessment instrument for ongoing evaluation.

Table 1, Summary of Foundation Experiences Adapting the McKinsey Capacity Assessment Grid (page 32), compares how three foundations used a McKinsey-based capacity assessment instrument, including highlights of the customized versions. Some grantmakers, such as SVP Seattle, made only minor changes to the original grid. Others, such as the CCI, created a highly customized version, using some questions from the original grid and many new ones created in the same format.

Background on the McKinsey Grid

While the sophistication of nonprofits' organizational systems has evolved significantly in the last decade, the tools for assessing and measuring capacity have not kept pace.[10] Assessments that rely on outside experts have the advantage of objectivity. However, there has been a growing interest in using self-assessment tools. Well-designed self-assessment tools can promote a greater sense of ownership in the assessment process and are less expensive to administer, making them more accessible to a wider range of nonprofits.

The McKinsey Capacity Assessment Grid grew out of research commissioned in 2001 by Venture Philanthropy Partners to identify successful nonprofit capacity-building experiences. The results, published in *Effective Capacity Building in Nonprofit Organizations,* presented a framework for conceptualizing different components of organizational capacity and included a self-assessment tool to help nonprofits identify their capacity strengths and weaknesses. The McKinsey Grid is a product of McKinsey & Company's managerial expertise and hundreds of hours of research and development.

---

[10] Evan Bloom, Meg Kinghorn, and Betsy Kummer, *Capacity Building Perspectives: Understanding Organizational Assessment* (Impact Alliance Connections, July 2003).

Table 1. Summary of Foundation Experiences Adapting the McKinsey Capacity Assessment Grid

This table provides a synopsis of how each foundation featured in this article used and adapted the McKinsey Capacity Assessment Grid.

Foundation	Goals for Assessing Capacity	Process Using the Grid	Modifications to Original McKinsey Grid
Social Venture Partners (SVP) Seattle Seattle, WA www.svpseattle.org Mid-size children's, education, and environmental nonprofits in the greater Seattle area	1. Help funder and nonprofit align goals and resources for annual capacity-building plans for individual grantees 2. Measure long-term growth in capacity and assess effectiveness of different capacity-building resources and strategies	Used first as part of a retrospective evaluation of its effectiveness in capacity building Currently administered annually to all 22 grantees and used to develop yearly capacity-building work plans	Created new questions on fundraising, communications and board issues Reorganized original questions into capacity taxonomy based on 10 skill areas Added method for nonprofits to prioritize capacity-building goals
Community Clinics Initiative (CCI) San Francisco, CA www.communityclinics.org Community clinics and health centers in California (a total universe of about 180 organizations)	1. Give a portrait of capacity strengths and weaknesses across the field 2. Stimulate dialog in the field about the importance of capacity 3. Provide an initial needs assessment baseline for long-term evaluation 4. Inform funder's program development	Delivered as optional tool in grant application to help clinics develop more informed requests for capacity-building grants Later administered to all grantees immediately after funding decisions made at beginning of new capacity-building program (90 respondents)	Developed highly customized 32-question survey to assess aspects of capacity related to capital campaigns Questions include mix of original McKinsey questions and many new questions specific to assessing funder's theory of change for their program as well as using already existing benchmarks of capacity specific to community clinics
Marguerite Casey Foundation Seattle, WA www.caseygrants.org Organizations working in advocacy and organizing, leadership development, public policy change, and cross-sector collaboration in regions of the country	1. Increase awareness of capacity issues among grantees 2. Deepen funder's understanding of the strengths and weaknesses in capacity across grantee portfolio 3. Identify potential opportunities for cross-grantee training and technical assistance	All grantees requested to complete assessment in 2004 (87% response rate) Foundation currently deciding how to use the instrument on an ongoing basis	Created new questions on organizing and constituency involvement Strengthened questions on evaluation, marketing, communications, and fundraising and dropped some McKinsey questions viewed as redundant or nonessential Edited language to be more culturally appropriate to community organizing and advocacy groups Reorganized questions into 4 dimensions of capacity Added method for nonprofit to prioritize capacity-building goals

The McKinsey Grid was designed to assess seven broad areas of capacity, with specific indicators under each category:

1. Aspirations

2. Strategy

3. Organizational skills

4. Human resources

5. Systems and infrastructure

6. Organizational structure

7. Culture

When reviewing potential capacity self-assessment tools for clients over the past few years, Blueprint found that the McKinsey Grid offered two important advantages over other tools in the field.

• It includes the most comprehensive set of questions and recognizes that organizational capacity includes higher-level elements of leadership, mission, and vision. (Many other assessment instruments focus primarily on technical and organizational skills.)

• Each question uses a four-level rating scale with detailed descriptions of activities that demonstrate capacity at each level. These descriptions ensure that a "Level 2" on any aspect of capacity means approximately the same thing across different respondents. These descriptions reduce subjectivity within an organization and increase the validity of comparing scores across nonprofits. Many other capacity assessment instruments include only lists of capacities with Yes-No check boxes. Tools that use numerical scales asked respondents to rate capacity elements on a numerical scale, but do not provide descriptors that define each level on the scale. Figure 2, Example of McKinsey Grid Question (page 34) provides an example of the McKinsey rating scale.

Figure 2. Example of McKinsey Grid Question

	1. Clear need for increased capacity	2. Basic level of capacity in place	3. Moderate level of capacity in place	4. High level of capacity in place
Mission	No written mission or limited expression of the organization's reason for existence (lacks clarity or specificity); either held by very few in the organization or rarely referenced	Some expression of organization's reason for existence that reflects its values and purpose, but may lack clarity; held by some within the organization and occasionally referenced	Clear expression of the organization's reason for existence that reflects its values and purpose; held by many within organization and often referenced	Clear expression of the organization's reason for existence that describes an enduring reality that reflects its values and purpose; universally held within organization and frequently referenced

Venture Philanthropy Partners retains the copyright on the McKinsey Capacity Assessment Grid. They have generously made the tool widely available to all nonprofits at no cost. They have also allowed grantmakers to customize the grid (without charge) to meet their unique needs if they request permission. This customization helps an already powerful tool evolve through practitioner use and feedback.

How the Assessment Process Works

A McKinsey-based capacity assessment instrument asks nonprofits to place themselves on a continuum for about sixty different aspects of capacity.[11] Ideally, the executive director, several key senior staff, and a board member complete the assessment tool independently. The instrument takes individuals sixty to ninety minutes to complete. (See the CD-ROM that accompanies this book for a copy of the original McKinsey Grid and the McKinsey-based capacity assessment instrument created for the Marguerite Casey Foundation in 2004, which is the most recent customization and builds on the lessons from the other grantmakers.)

---

[11] The number of questions depends on which version of the tool is being used. Also, some grantmakers have chosen to regroup the questions into a different taxonomy of capacity. See Recommendations for Customizing the McKinsey Grid (page 48) for more details.

Participants can then share scores with one another and meet to discuss differences in their ratings. If they are submitting scores to a foundation, they should align on a single set of results. The amount of time required for the entire assessment process ranges from four to fifteen hours, depending on the number of participants and meetings. Once all elements are rated, Blueprint found it helpful to ask nonprofits to review a summary of their scores across all areas and identify the elements of capacity that are their greatest priority for strengthening in the next one to two years.[12]

The most common challenge for grantees in completing the assessment was the difficulty of scoring themselves when they felt they did not exactly meet all the criteria of any one level. The rating system was designed as a "temperature check," not a rigid benchmarking scale, and nonprofits should be encouraged to choose the description that fits best.

Reasons Grantmakers Might Conduct a Capacity Assessment

The grantmakers who used the McKinsey Grid were motivated by one or more of the following four goals:

1. Enhance grantees' understanding of their own organizational capacity and serve as a catalyst for action

2. Increase funder knowledge about grantee capacity

3. Inform technical assistance plans and marshal new resources

4. Track growth over time

1. Enhance grantees' understanding of their own organizational capacity and serve as a catalyst for action

Grantees at all three foundations overwhelmingly viewed capacity assessment as a valuable organizational development exercise. Many grantees said the process of completing the assessment expanded their knowledge because it drew attention to components of capacity they may not have considered. For many less-developed nonprofits, it provided a vision of what higher capacity would

---

[12] This prioritization step is not part of the original McKinsey Capacity Assessment Grid.

look like. The assessment instrument also provided nonprofit staff with a common framework and vocabulary for talking about organizational capacity, both among themselves and with their funder. When multiple staff and board members participate, the assessment process also stimulates critical dialog on capacity.

Many nonprofits valued the assessment process primarily as an inspiration for action rather than as a way to identify new issues. Even when the instrument did not identify any big surprises, nonprofits said it was useful to highlight capacity issues that at least some staff felt had been bubbling under the surface unacknowledged. A number of grantees reported that the process spurred them to take some action to improve capacity needs identified through the assessment process—even though the funder did not require any action. Others planned to use the results at upcoming staff or board retreats. A few planned to use it in an ongoing manner, either for benchmarking or for their own internal evaluation.

Grantees on the Assessment Process

Following are comments from some grantees who participated in the assessments.[13]

"I love this tool! I think it's one of the best things since sliced bread . . . I can't tell you how happy this makes me. What you have done is given a standard. Six years ago I said I wanted to be the best nonprofit in New Orleans. But what does that look like? How do you assess it? How do you say 'we are the best because . . .' This tool gives us a standard."

— *Executive director of a nonprofit*
in New Orleans

"What this has done is laid our weaknesses out in such a nice neat little package, especially the summary chart, and gives us some meat to talk about it with the board."

— *Executive director of a hunger*
coalition in the Southeast

"The staff/board conversations around aligning [on a single set of ratings] was the most valuable part of the process. It evoked an increased level of self-consciousness about our organization and required us to clarify our assumptions."

— *Codirector of an antiracism*
organization in California

"Our board is going through a growing process and the tool helped them think about whom else they need [to recruit], with what skills, backgrounds, ethnicities. Through the process of completing the tool, we have asked one of board members who has background in diversity issues to focus on diversity issues for our organization."

— *Board member of child-serving*
agency in San Francisco

[13] These comments were collected during confidential telephone interviews with a sample of the McKinsey Foundation's grantees conducted after they had completed the assessment process. Details have been changed to protect confidentiality.

2. Increase funder knowledge about grantee capacity

The grantmakers use data from their assessment instruments to better understand grantee capacity at three levels:

- The individual grantee
- Cohorts of grantees
- An entire field of nonprofits

SVP Seattle uses information on individual grantees to develop appropriate goals and expectations for each organization. Unlike some of the other capacity assessment tools, a McKinsey-based capacity assessment instrument also can provide a portrait of capacity across a group of grantees, even those doing different kinds of work. The Marguerite Casey Foundation used its data to understand overall strengths and weaknesses among its grantee portfolio as well as to identify regional differences in capacity-building priorities. For example, a key finding indicated that grantees with a national focus place a much higher priority on improving their strategic planning capacity than do organizations with a regional focus. And while grantees' capacity scores did not vary significantly by region, grantees in the South placed a much higher priority on improving their evaluation skills than those in other regions. In contrast, grantees in the Southwest showed a strong consensus around the priority to strengthen their fundraising skills.

The Community Clinics Initiative (CCI), a funder trying to build the capacity of a field of mission-aligned organizations, used its data to create a portrait of organizational capacity across all community clinics and health centers in California. It found that clinics consider their strongest areas of capacity to be leadership in their management team, their financial systems and position, and community engagement and collaboration. Clinics consider their weakest areas of capacity to be fund development, data-informed decision-making, and leadership within their boards of directors. CCI is using a report on the composite portrait of its grantees to stimulate dialog among clinics as well as their infrastructure organizations and other funders about the field's capacity needs and how to address them in a more comprehensive fashion.

3. Inform technical assistance plans and marshal new resources

The portrait of grantee capacity becomes a natural springboard for planning a capacity-building intervention, whether for an individual grantee or across a cohort. SVP Seattle uses annual capacity assessments to help develop individualized capacity-building plans for each of its grantees. The capacity assessment process is especially valuable with new grantees. Before it started using the McKinsey Grid in 2003, SVP Seattle found that it could take more than a year for a nonprofit and funder to align on the grantee's most important needs and the best ways for SVP to help.[14]

Understanding the capacity of a cohort of grantees can help grantmakers identify opportunities for group training and other ways to maximize their work across the cohort. The composite assessment for the Marguerite Casey Foundation uncovered regional differences in grantee priorities for capacity strengthening. CCI's portrait is shaping the way it provides support for strengthening fund development capacity. The portrait also identified areas of need outside its funding guidelines, such as board leadership. CCI is using the report to encourage other funders to focus on these areas.

4. Track growth over time

Although the McKinsey Grid was originally designed as a diagnostic tool, a number of grantmakers are exploring how it can be used to measure growth in organizational capacity over time. Several SVP affiliates, including SVP Seattle, intend to use scores to help grantees measure their progress over time. However, because real capacity growth takes several years, no affiliate has used the instrument long enough to test its validity as a measurement instrument over time. Most significantly, the grid only distinguishes four levels of competency in each area, and therefore is not sensitive enough to note many significant capacity changes.

Several grantmakers have used the McKinsey Grid as part of a retrospective assessment of their capacity-building work across grantees. SVP Seattle used the grid as one piece of data in assessing its first five years of capacity-building work.[15] They asked grantees to identify both their current level of

---

[14] K. Guthrie, A. Preston, and L. Bernholz, *Transforming Philanthropic Transactions: An Evaluation of the First Five Years of Social Venture Partners Seattle* (Seattle, WA: Social Venture Partners, 2003).
[15] Ibid.

capacity and their level at the beginning of the relationship with the funder. While retrospective assessment of capacity is subject to the vicissitudes of people's memories, it also offers nonprofits some advantages, particularly if the executive director and/or board chair have remained constant. Specifically, in some cases, nonprofit staff may not fully appreciate some of the deficiencies in their capacity until they have experienced stronger capacity. [16]

Finally, grantmakers can use the composite portraits of grantee capacity to set program-level goals for their own capacity building. For example, foundations could commit to helping all their grantees reach a minimum level of capacity or to raise the average capacity levels in certain key areas over a defined time period.

Lessons Learned about Successful Implementation

The grantmakers Blueprint has worked with have learned several lessons that can help with successful implementation of such tools:

- View capacity assessment tools as a way to assist grantees, rather than to judge them
- Nonprofits should approach the assessment as a process rather than a survey
- Involve board members
- Tie the assessment to an organizational planning and goal-setting process
- Don't assume that capacity areas with the lowest scores are the highest priorities for grantees
- Time the assessment process to advance funder goals and the grantee-funder relationship

---

[16] The Robin Hood Foundation in New York City also recently used a McKinsey-based tool as part of an internally conducted retrospective evaluation of their capacity-building work.

Creating a Portrait of Capacity Across a Group

Grantmakers can create a composite portrait of the organizational capacity across a cohort of grantees by two methods—averaging or proportioning.

Averaging creates a single composite portrait for the group by calculating the mean score across all grantees on each of the approximately sixty individual capacity elements. Viewing composite capacity scores by averaging provides funders with a quick read on strengths and weaknesses of different capacities across the cohort. However, averaging can mask important differences in the distribution of strength within an element.

The *proportioning* method more accurately reflects the nature of the data and shows the distribution of strength in any individual capacity element across a group of grantees. In this method, one calculates the proportion of grantees at each of the four levels of strength for each of the approximately sixty capacity elements, giving each individual question in the grid four data points. However, the volume of data in this method can be overwhelming, making it difficult to identify patterns. Therefore, Blueprint has found it useful to look at a single set of data using both methods. Chart 1 and Chart 2 show the same data displayed in the two different ways. Chart 1 uses averaging; Chart 2 shows the same data using the proportional method.

Chart 1. Viewing Composite Capacity Scores by Averaging

Chart 1 shows that averaging across nonprofits provides a quick read on strengths and weaknesses of different capacities across the cohort.

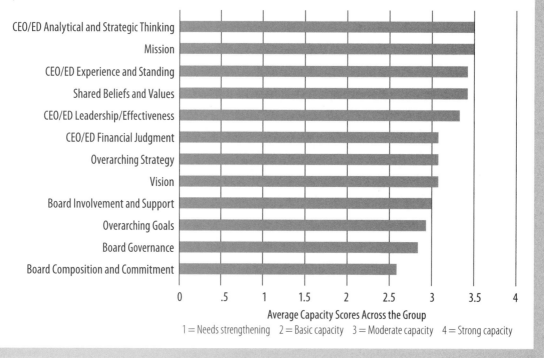

1 = Needs strengthening   2 = Basic capacity   3 = Moderate capacity   4 = Strong capacity

Chart 2. Viewing Composite Capacity Scores by the Proportioning Method

Chart 2 uses the same data as Chart 1, but applies the proportioning method. The proportioning method highlights the distribution of capacity strength for each element across the grantee population.

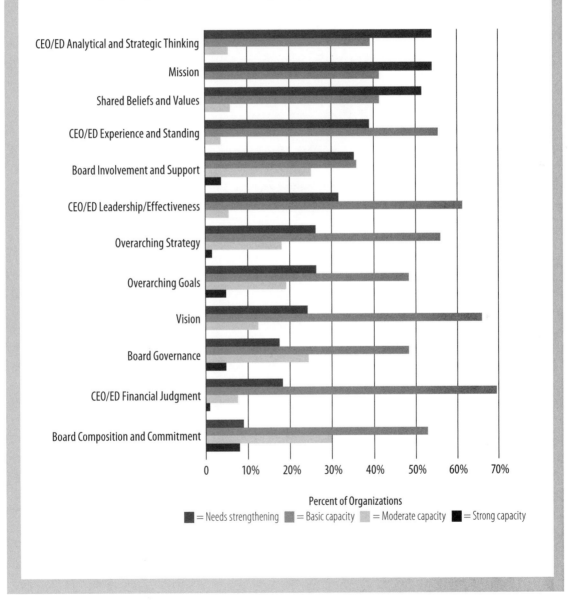

Percent of Organizations

■ = Needs strengthening   ■ = Basic capacity   ■ = Moderate capacity   ■ = Strong capacity

View capacity assessment tools as a way to assist grantees, rather than to judge them

Nonprofits interviewed across the three foundations voiced concern about how funders might use the assessment data, particularly if they saw scores for individual grantees. One stated, "The foundation really needs to be clear on whether this is a helping tool or a judging tool." Grantees said they would be much more honest about their capacity when they felt assured that the funder viewed the assessment process as a vehicle to help grantees improve their capacity. If the assessment results were used in connection with funding decisions, there would be incentive to inflate scores. So far, SVP Seattle, CCI, and the Marguerite Casey Foundation all have separated the assessment process from funding decisions. CCI and the Marguerite Casey Foundation mitigated this issue further by having nonprofits submit their assessment scores to an independent evaluator who shared summary results only with the foundations. SVP Seattle dealt with the concern by viewing grantee scores only *after* initial funding decisions are made and grantees are developing their first work plan. Ongoing grantees are required to submit their annual assessments as part of refunding decisions. However, SVP believes that its high degree of engagement with its grantees creates a base of trust that allows grantees to be candid in their assessments.

Grantmakers could increase the incentive for honesty by making monetary support or technical assistance available to grantees that identify areas they want to work on. "If someone wants to help me with my weaknesses, I will tell them all of my dirty laundry," said one grantee. SVP Seattle is explicit in presenting the instrument as an aid for the grantee and funder to identify the combination of SVP resources best suited to helping the grantee strengthen its capacity. More accurate assessments lead to better-targeted resources.

Nonprofits should approach the assessment as a process rather than a survey

Nonprofits that approached the assessment as a process viewed the experience more favorably than those that viewed it as a survey. The greatest insights for organizations tended to surface when multiple staff members completed the assessment independently, then shared results and discussed their differences.[17]

---

[17] In many cases, nonprofits had the executive director fill out the survey and then pass it around for comments. This approach makes it harder for staff to voice contradictory opinions.

Foundations found that they achieved better results when they introduced the assessment process to grantees and stressed the importance of taking the time to include a wide range of staff and board members in the process. Some foundations found that paying a small stipend made it more likely that the nonprofits would engage a wider range of people in the process. The Marguerite Casey Foundation provided a $250 stipend to all grantees completing the assessment. The stipend generated tremendous goodwill and contributed to a remarkable 87 percent response rate.

Involve board members

Involving board members in the assessment process is challenging but especially valuable. Many board members are initially drawn to an organization for its programs and can be reluctant to invest resources in capacity building. Completing the instrument stimulates dialog and can educate board members in a nonthreatening way about the importance of organizational capacity as well as their own role in issues such as fundraising. Assessments of the executive director and senior leadership team may be more accurate with input from one or more board members.

All three foundations asked their grantees to involve board members. However, the Marguerite Casey Foundation and CCI found that less than half the grantees incorporated board member input. Many nonprofits expressed reluctance to even ask board members for input. Reasons cited included board member disinterest, and concern about using the board members' limited time for something that may not be the nonprofit's top priority. Funders and executive directors should work together to develop better ways to solicit board involvement, perhaps through a shortened version of the instrument and greater outreach.

Tie the assessment to an organizational planning and goal-setting process

The assessment process is most useful when an organization ties the results directly to its planning process rather than viewing it as a stand-alone activity. SVP Seattle explicitly tells grantees to use the data from their assessments to shape their annual capacity-building plans and requests for SVP resources to support them. See Table 2, Sample Organizational Capacity-building Goals and Objectives, for an example of how an SVP Seattle grantee used data from a capacity assessment to develop goals and objectives—essentially converting the assessment process into a capacity-building opportunity.

Table 2. Sample Organizational Capacity-Building Goals and Objectives

Goal Area	Goal	Objective
Board Leadership	Restructure board of directors and membership to improve overall performance	Adjust board practices based on nonprofit board best practices, strategic plan, and results of board retreat, with goal of increasing board attendance at meetings (at least 80%), clarifying/changing committee and board member roles, and increasing diversity of skill sets among members. Identify and prioritize three roles that need to be filled by new members and three goals for board development. Present updated practices plan at June board meeting.
Mission, Vision, Strategy	Develop long-range strategic plan	Finalize three-year strategic plan with input from at least six Advisory Board members, SVP lead partner, and SVP volunteer and consultant.
Fund Development	Diversify funding to create sustainable revenue stream	Develop fundraising plan with input from Advisory Board Finance Committee members, SVP lead partner, and SVP volunteer.
Leadership Development	Develop director's management skills	Director will meet with leadership/executive coaching volunteer once per month (phone or in person) to monitor improvement in areas of communicating vision "above and below," dealing with difficult situations, and developing staff.
Marketing & Communications	Increase Investee A's name recognition and reputation as an outstanding program for underserved youth	Work with SVP volunteer or consultant and another volunteer to develop a marketing plan that will increase our presence in specific communities, strengthen our relationships with district and state K–12 institutions, and improve our ability to form partnerships and increase our funding.
Program Design & Evaluation	Build on our prior learning about program	Develop formative evaluation plan for two additional programs, using Ninth Grade Bridge materials as a model.

Don't assume that capacity areas with the lowest scores are the highest priorities for grantees

Both SVP Seattle and the Marguerite Casey Foundation found that grantee priorities for capacity building were not always the same as areas where scores from the assessment tool were lowest. For example, among grantees of the Marguerite Casey Foundation, the capacities with the lowest overall scores were board involvement in fundraising and human resources planning—but only a few of the grantees cited these areas as priorities for strengthening. This point highlights the fact that lower levels of capacity in some areas may not be problematic for some nonprofits at certain stages in their development. Developing technical assistance plans requires balancing what the assessment instrument would suggest are areas most in need of strengthening with grantees' own priorities for improving their capacity.

Time the assessment process to advance funder goals and the grantee-funder relationship

Funders have several options for the timing of a capacity assessment:

- Make it part of the grant application process
- Assess at the beginning of a grant
- Assess at some point during the grant relationship after establishing some trust between grantee and grantor
- Assess at the conclusion of a grant

SVP Seattle finds the process most useful at the start of their relationship with a grantee. Because they have three- to five-year relationships with most grantees, SVP Seattle also expects grantees to check on their capacity assessment annually and then conduct another systematic assessment at the close of a grant. As a new foundation, Marguerite Casey collected its capacity data about a year after its first grants were awarded—after building some trust with grantees but still early enough to use the data to inform the foundation's program development. CCI conducted its assessment when it moved into building capacity more broadly (it had previously only given grants to increase information technology capacity) and used the assessment data to inform program planning. CCI also used a more limited version of the assessment as a voluntary part of the grant application process.

Lessons Learned about Interpreting Assessment Data

When using data from these self-assessments, grantmakers and grantees should keep in mind the following challenges and caveats:

- Self-assessment data is subjective
- A McKinsey-based assessment tool can measure only broad differences in capacity, not small variations
- There are challenges associated with measuring capacity growth over time
- Customizing the tool for each foundation can make rolling up and/or comparing data across foundations difficult

Self-assessment data is subjective

Respondents' answers are influenced by those people who participate in the assessment, their level of knowledge about the organization, and their desire to be perceived in a particular way. Compared to other self-assessments, the McKinsey Grid counters subjectivity bias by including detailed descriptions of capacity at each level and involving multiple people in completing the assessment process. CCI and the Marguerite Casey Foundation also tried to reduce the incentive for rating inflation by keeping scores anonymous to the foundation. Nonetheless, a level of subjectivity will always be inherent in any self-assessment and, therefore, scores should not be treated as an objective or scientific measure of capacity.

A McKinsey-based assessment tool can measure only broad differences in capacity, not small variations

Small differences in capacity won't be detected by a McKinsey-based assessment tool. The instrument asks respondents to choose along a 4-point scale for each capacity element, rather than a 10-point or 100-point scale. While this approach makes it easier for respondents to complete the tool, it also means that, when comparing capacity scores between organizations, only major differences will be captured.[18] Because the instrument cannot differentiate among

---

[18] Blueprint conducted some pilot tests with an expanded 12-point scale in an attempt to get more variation for statistical purposes, but nonprofits found it overly complex for their own assessment purposes.

respondents that have small differences in capacity, finding statistical relationships between capacity scores and other quantitative variables, such as organizational budget size, is much more challenging. Blueprint has found it most useful to look at scores in capacity building in relationship to each other. It placed composite capacity scores in rank order from high to low, which highlighted areas where most organizations saw themselves as especially strong or especially weak.

There are challenges associated with measuring capacity growth over time

Given the limited ability for the assessment tool to measure small differences or small changes in capacity, and the complexities of the concepts being measured, it would be unrealistic to expect a McKinsey-based capacity instrument to pick up changes in grantee capacity on an annual basis. Most capacity growth takes at least three years to materialize. No foundation has used a McKinsey-based capacity instrument long enough to test its effectiveness in measuring growth in capacity over a longer time period. Moreover, staff changes may affect the validity of any assessment over time because new people may assess the organization's capacity somewhat differently than the previous respondents. It may be more appropriate to measure growth across a large pool of grantees than at an individual grantee level. While many foundations yearn for a more scientific tool for measuring capacity, McKinsey-based assessment instruments are, perhaps, more appropriately viewed as a grading framework than a scientific measurement instrument.

Customizing the tool for each foundation can make rolling up and/or comparing data across foundations difficult

While each foundation has a desire to customize the questions for its specific needs, one cost is reducing the ability to directly compare across foundations. At this point, the three versions of the McKinsey Grid created for the funders highlighted in this chapter are so different that it is difficult to make direct quantitative comparisons across grantees from different foundations. Some foundations with a strong interest in capacity building would like to see the field align on a core, common set of questions about the most generalizable elements of capacity building. This standardization would allow data to be pooled across many more grantees and support cross-foundation efforts to explore how capacity growth leads to better client outcomes.

Recommendations for Customizing the McKinsey Grid

Blueprint customized the McKinsey Grid for each of the three funders featured in this chapter based on each foundation's goals and feedback from grantees. Over the course of several years, Blueprint has tested six key enhancements that would be valuable for any customization effort.

- Reorganize the questions around a more intuitive taxonomy
- Add questions that assess areas of capacity underrepresented in the original McKinsey Grid
- Add a mechanism for organizations to identify their capacity-building priorities
- Edit the language to resonate with a wider range of nonprofits
- Use an electronic format
- Develop new questions that are relevant to specific groups of nonprofits

The Marguerite Casey version, included in the CD-ROM that accompanies this book, is the most recent Blueprint adaptation and incorporates all of these enhancements. Table 3 lists the capacity elements covered in the tool, sorted according to the new taxonomy. It identifies new questions developed for the Marguerite Casey Foundation.

Reorganize the questions around a more intuitive taxonomy

McKinsey's original taxonomy of organizational capacity was an important advancement when it was introduced because it sensitized nonprofits (and capacity builders) to the importance of higher-level aspects of capacity such as vision, culture, and leadership. However, many nonprofits told Blueprint that they found the taxonomy hard to explain to staff and that categories were difficult to translate into concrete work plans. SVP Seattle rearranged the original McKinsey questions under a 10-item taxonomy that aligned with the functional areas in which their grantees typically seek technical assistance.[19] For the Marguerite Casey Foundation, Blueprint employed a framework of four dimensions of nonprofit organizational capacity—leadership, adaptive, management, and operational—that was developed by the TCC Group during its research on management support organizations.[20] The Marguerite Casey Taxonomy and associated questions are listed in Table 3 (page 50). Future users of a McKinsey-based assessment tool might consider either of the taxonomies described above or develop a taxonomy that specifically aligns with their program's theory of change, as did CCI. Existing questions for specific capacity elements can be reorganized into one of the existing taxonomies or a new one.

Add questions that assess areas of capacity underrepresented in the original McKinsey Grid

Several foundations found that the original McKinsey Grid questions did not adequately cover some aspects of capacity they had found to be important. Multiple grantmakers expressed an interest in collecting more data on fundraising, marketing/communications and board involvement. Blueprint developed new questions in these areas for all three foundations highlighted in this chapter.

---

[19] These dimensions are Mission, Vision & Planning; Program Design & Evaluation; Human Resources; CEO/Senior Management Leadership Team; Information Technology; Financial Management; Fund Development; Board Leadership; Legal Affairs; and Marketing, Communications & External Relations.

[20] Categories adapted from P. Connolly and P. York, *Building the Capacity of Capacity Builders: A Study of Management Support and Field-building Organizations in the Nonprofit Sector* (New York: The TCC Group [formerly the Conservation Company], June 2003).

Table 3. Outline of the Marguerite Casey Capacity Assessment

This table lists the broad dimension of organizational capacity and associated capacity elements (or question topics) used in the foundation's McKinsey-based capacity assessment tool. New questions developed for the Marguerite Casey Foundation are listed in italic. Questions in regular typeface come from the original McKinsey Grid, although some of their wording may have been adapted.

Leadership Capacity		Adaptive Capacity		Management Capacity		Operational Capacity	
1.01	Mission	2.01	Strategic Planning	3.01	Senior Management Team	4.01	Staffing Levels
1.02	Vision	2.02	*Evaluation/Performance Measurement*	3.02	Staff	4.02	*Skills, Abilities, & Commitment of Volunteers*
1.03	Overarching Goals	2.03	*Evaluation & Organizational Learning*	3.03	Dependence of Management Team & Staff on CEO/ED	4.03	Fundraising
1.04	Overarching Strategy	2.04	*Use of Research Data to Support Program Planning & Advocacy*	3.04	Shared References & Practices	4.04	*Board Involvement & Participation in Fundraising*
1.05	Shared Beliefs & Values	2.05	Program Relevance & Integration	3.05	Goals/Performance Targets	4.05	Revenue Generation
1.06	Board Composition & Commitment	2.06	Program Growth & Replication	3.06	Funding Model	4.06	*Communications Strategy*
1.07	Board Governance	2.07	New Program Development	3.07	*Fund Development Planning*	4.07	*Communications & Outreach*
1.08	Board Involvement & Support	2.08	Monitoring of Program Landscape	3.08	Financial Planning / Budgeting	4.08	Telephone & Fax
1.09	CEO/ED Experience & Standing	2.09	*Assessment of External Environment & Community Needs*	3.09	Financial Operations Management	4.09	Computers, Applications, Network, & E-mail
1.10	CEO/ED Organizational Leadership/Effectiveness	2.10	Influencing of Policy Making	3.10	Operational Planning	4.10	Web Site
1.11	CEO/ED Analytical & Strategic Thinking	2.11	Partnerships & Alliances	3.11	Organizational Processes	4.11	Databases / Management Reporting Systems
1.12	CEO/ED Financial Judgment	2.12	*Community Presence & Standing*	3.12	Decision-making Processes	4.12	Buildings & Office Space
1.13	*Board & CEO/ED Appreciation of Power Issues*	2.13	*Constituent Involvement*	3.13	Knowledge Management	4.13	Management of Legal & Liability Matters
1.14	*Ability to Motivate & Mobilize Constituents*	2.14	*Organizing*	3.14	Interfunctional Coordination & Communication		
				3.15	Human Resources Planning		
				3.16	Recruiting, Development, & Retention of Management		
				3.17	Recruiting, Development, & Retention of General Staff		
				3.18	*Volunteer Management*		

Add a mechanism for organizations to identify their capacity-building priorities

On the summary page of the assessment instrument, Blueprint added a step where the nonprofit selects its top three to four priorities for capacity building. This step encourages nonprofits to use the assessment results to start setting goals and developing action plans. Grantmakers also found the prioritization data valuable when designing technical assistance plans for grantees because grantees' highest priorities weren't always the same as their lowest scoring areas. Several grantees of SVP and Marguerite Casey recommended that future versions of the tool take this planning process further. This might include developing an additional worksheet to more explicitly guide nonprofits through translating their assessment results and priorities into specific action plans.

Edit the language to resonate with a wider range of nonprofits

McKinsey developed the original grid while working with a set of highly engaged capacity-building grantmakers who strongly emphasized performance measures and bringing business practices to nonprofits. Although McKinsey worked hard to avoid business jargon, a number of nonprofits interviewed by Blueprint still found the language and assumptions in some of the questions off-putting. For example, the questions about board composition were viewed by many as biased in favor of "high-profile" members, whereas many community-based organizations favor community activists and constituents on their boards. Blueprint worked with Marguerite Casey grantees and a local expert in cultural competency to ensure that the language in their survey was appropriate for both large nonprofits and smaller, ethnically diverse advocacy organizations.

Use an electronic format

Blueprint created a Microsoft Excel version of the assessment grid in which respondents recorded their ratings in an Excel workbook that automatically tabulates capacity ratings and generates a summary table and chart. This summary provides a nonprofit with immediate feedback on its strengths and weaknesses. The electronic format also makes it easier to pass around to colleagues or paste into proposals. Finally, it allows a nonprofit to submit scores to funders or outside evaluators electronically, which speeds up data compilation for those wanting a composite portrait of a group of grantees. A copy of the Excel workbook is on the CD accompanying this book.

Develop new questions that are relevant to specific groups of nonprofits

Foundations that fund organizations with a highly focused niche may want to develop questions specific to that niche, as did CCI and the Marguerite Casey Foundation. For example, the Marguerite Casey Foundation has a particular focus on funding community organizing and advocacy nonprofits. Some aspects of capacity particular to these activities are not reflected in the original McKinsey Grid. Blueprint developed a series of questions to assess these capacities.

Summary

The McKinsey Capacity Assessment Grid is a powerful tool, valuable to both individual nonprofits wanting to systematically assess their own capacity and to funders seeking to better understand the capacity-building needs of their grantees. McKinsey and Venture Philanthropy Partners should be commended for their foresight in developing this instrument and sharing it with the field.

The experiences here show that the instrument has the flexibility to meet the needs of different types of funders. The key for grantmakers is to identify their goals, then design a process and customize the tool to support them. There is tremendous value in continuing to refine both the instrument and the process to maximize the impact of this asset to the capacity-building field. The suggestions contained herein can contribute to continued enhancements of the grid, as can the knowledge gleaned by others who have applied the instrument in their work.

About the Grantmakers

Community Clinics Initiative

http://www.communityclinics.org

Community Clinics Initiative (CCI)[21] seeks to strengthen the role of community clinics in California as key social change organizations engaged in building stronger and healthier communities. CCI's mission is to help increase the organizational capacity of individual clinics and also to build the capacity of the field. We have a defined target audience of 180 clinic corporations and twenty regional networks of these clinics.

Beginning in 1999 with a grantmaking program in technology development, CCI learned that successful implementation of complex projects depended on strong internal organizational capacity. In 2002, a new grant program was created to specifically support capacity building and capital development.

Capacity assessment goals

With the beginning of the capacity-building program, CCI needed a systematic way to understand the state of organizational capacity across the field to first, engage grantees in a conversation about the importance of organizational capacity building, and second, inform our program development. Over time, our goals were to build knowledge of what combinations and levels of organizational capacities underpin successful programs and projects.

To promote grantee knowledge about capacity, we began by asking all applicants for the initial round of capacity-building grants to complete a pilot version of an assessment as part of their proposal development process. We did not require grantees to submit the results, but the proposal application did ask them to reflect on the process and use their insights to justify their request. Those applicants that cited their use of the assessment delivered stronger requests for capacity-building support. The pilot version of the assessment was so successful that we had our evaluators create an expanded version and asked any clinic that had ever received a grant from CCI to complete it. For program

---

[21] CCI is a joint project of the Tides Foundation and the California Endowment.

development purposes, we needed data about the field of community clinics as a whole rather than information about individual grantees. Because we did not need to know the assessment scores of individual grantees, grantees submitted scores directly to the evaluator.

Previous program evaluation data had already revealed the key elements that make clinic organizations strong (leadership, mission, community engagement, agility). But we did not know where clinics fell on the development continuum of those elements. And we had no data to guide decisions about which capacities to focus on developing in clinics. The capacity assessment instrument seemed a perfect vehicle to collect the information that CCI needed as a funder while sparking discussion about areas that needed attention and training, both at the clinic level and throughout the field.

Customizations made

While community clinics and health centers are similar to other nonprofits, there are also some distinct differences, given the nature of community clinics' work, their regulatory and funding complexities, and their size (even a small clinic has a budget of $1 million). Therefore, we designed a capacity assessment tool specifically for community health centers and clinics, drawing on the original McKinsey Grid questions when relevant and creating new questions on issues important to our program using a few existing benchmarks for clinic performance.

Outcomes

Grantees have reported informally that one of the greatest unexpected benefits of the assessment instrument is the articulation of standards. Grantee clinics have told us that the instrument's explicit descriptions of capacity at each level represented the clearest articulation of what capabilities they should be striving toward. Many noted that previous funders have urged organizations to improve (cultivate a stronger board, deepen their management team, or to plan more strategically), but never provided specific guidance on what improvement would look like.

The results of the compiled assessments have informed our program development and focus. While certain elements were presumed to be strong and others presumed to be weak, the assessment also identified unexpected areas of strength and weakness. These findings prompted some course corrections to CCI's capacity-building work.

Sharing the results of the assessment process has been a key component of our capacity-building strategy. In 2004, CCI released the results of the first capacity assessment in a report to the field to further stimulate public conversation among clinics, their infrastructure organizations, and other funders about the importance of capacity-building and areas of weakness and of strength.

Community Clinics Initiative intends to re-administer the assessment over time as part of our program evaluation. While any progress made will not be directly causal, the results should point to heightened awareness of levels of capacity and a movement upwards by the field as a whole.

A copy of the CCI capacity assessment tool as well as a report on the evaluation findings can be found on the CD accompanying this text and at http://www.communityclinics.org/section/library

Marguerite Casey Foundation

http://www.caseygrants.org

Marguerite Casey Foundation is dedicated to supporting a movement of low-income families who advocate on their own behalf for change. The foundation strives to achieve this through respectful, thoughtful grantmaking based on continual learning and reflection.

A tenet of Marguerite Casey Foundation's approach to evaluation is that any activity should have dual utility: both for the foundation and our grantees. As part of this commitment, we have undertaken a multifaceted approach to evaluation, which includes asking grantee organizations to complete a capacity assessment tool.

Capacity assessment goals

The foundation had two objectives in implementing a capacity assessment instrument. The first was to help our grantees gain a better understanding of their own capacity and to set goals for strengthening it. The second was to provide information on grantees' capacity to inform foundation staff and board decision making around program planning and evaluation.

Customizations made

The foundation modified the language and structure of the McKinsey Capacity Assessment Grid to better match the needs of our grantees, which are primarily community-based advocacy organizations. To encourage candidness, and because aggregate data would be sufficient for our purposes, we decided to "blind" individual organizational capacity ratings. The foundation's evaluator collected scores from individual grantees and submitted the aggregate data to us, after analyzing the data regionally to complement our regional grantmaking strategy.

Outcomes

The Marguerite Casey Foundation is a young foundation, and the capacity assessment instrument has provided baseline information to help us understand the aggregate capacity strengths and weaknesses of our grantees. While due diligence is clearly of primary importance, this information is useful in building a snapshot of our grantees as a group. We will also use the information provided by the assessment to help craft our collective capacity-building plan, particularly in the foundation's subregions, and to better understand how we can support a group of movement-building organizations. As a foundation that primarily structures its grants as core operating support, we strive to better understand and measure the effectiveness and development of grantee organizations. The data provided by the assessment allows the foundation to better understand how funds might help strengthen grantee organizations as a group and increase their collective capacity to help families create change.

Marguerite Casey Foundation has a two-pronged approach around the future use of our capacity assessment instrument. First, we expect to ask grantee organizations to complete the assessment periodically and compare the data against the results of the 2004 survey. This should help us track the growth of the capacity areas over time and give a snapshot of where grantees as a group are at a specific point. Second, a select group of cornerstone grantee organizations, with whom the foundation has a long-term relationship, will be asked to complete the assessment instrument every few years and then discuss their individual capacity ratings. This will allow us to focus technical assistance efforts for those grantees and to better understand how large cornerstone organizations function.

One important thing we learned through this field test is the primary utility of board member and executive director involvement in the assessment process. Organizations that were able to engage multiple members of their leadership in the process found the activity much more useful and productive. However, less than half of the organizations were able to include one or more board members in the process. As we move forward, we will focus on how to increase the percentage of grantees that engage their board members in the process, making the assessment as useful as possible.

A copy of the Marguerite Casey capacity assessment tool can be found on the CD accompanying this book and at http://www.caseygrants.org/pages/resources/resources_downloadassessment.asp.

Social Venture Partners Seattle

http://www.svpseattle.org

Social Venture Partners (SVP) Seattle was founded in 1997 with the mission of promoting philanthropy and volunteerism to achieve positive social change in the Puget Sound region. SVP Seattle engages individual philanthropists in contributing their financial resources and expertise to support nonprofits working with children's issues, K–12 education, and the environment. We work with nonprofits to build their organizational capacity by providing cash grants, skilled volunteers, professional consultants, leadership development, and management training opportunities. We refer to our grantees as "investees" to reflect the long-term (three to five years), intensive nature of our partnerships.

Capacity assessment goals

SVP Seattle began using the McKinsey Capacity Assessment Grid with investees in 2003 in the hope that it would improve our understanding of the capacity-building needs of individual investees and to more effectively plan and measure the impact of capacity-building support across SVP's portfolio.[22] First, we wanted to provide investees with a framework to stimulate dialog about capacity building. SVP requires all investees to submit annual work plans that include program development and delivery goals, as well as capacity-building goals and objectives. The McKinsey Grid provided a robust methodology to help our grantees discuss, assess, and prioritize their capacity-building needs. Since using the assessment, investees have produced more sophisticated, targeted work plans.

We also hoped the McKinsey Grid would provide SVP with a macro-level understanding of the capacity-building needs of our investee portfolio. Data from investee assessments would allow us to analyze our portfolio by cohort, such as organization size, length of SVP relationship, or programmatic focus. Through analysis of the assessment results, we've identified capacity variances and trends in our portfolio. Accordingly, we have developed technical assistance and capacity-building interventions in areas where investees collectively had the greatest need for capacity building. In short, the assessment process helped SVP plan our capacity-building support in a more responsive and strategic way.

SVP also looked to the McKinsey Grid as a way to measure change in capacity over time. Prior to adopting the McKinsey Grid, we lacked a standardized and systematic way of knowing whether investees were indeed becoming stronger, more sustainable organizations. The tool provided a way to measure this from one year to the next, and from one organization to the next. Over a multiyear period, we also hoped to establish a correlation between SVP's inputs (grants, technical assistance, volunteers, paid consultants, and training opportunities) and the capacity gains of investees. While we cannot establish a causal relationship, we can certainly better understand the capacity areas where we are likely to have the most impact.

---

[22] The SVP model has been adopted in twenty-two cities and regions across the United States and Canada. Currently, four other SVP affiliates are using a derivative version of the McKinsey Grid, and four additional affiliates are in the process of determining whether and how the McKinsey Grid might be used with their investee portfolio.

Customizations made

SVP customized the McKinsey Grid in two ways. First, we altered the taxonomy used in the original McKinsey Grid. When crafting work plans, investees not only outline capacity-building goals but also define the areas where SVP's volunteer or paid consulting support will be sought. Historically, investees made requests using a framework of ten key skills. This taxonomy was familiar to SVP investees and seemed more intuitive than the original McKinsey Grid framework. We maintained all of the McKinsey questions but regrouped them according to these ten functional areas. This reorganization increased alignment between the assessment instrument, work plans, and our existing internal system for tracking and responding to volunteer or paid consultant requests.

Second, we created four new questions to assess aspects of capacity we found to be important but that were not adequately represented in the original grid. These questions covered fund development planning, board involvement in fundraising, communications strategy, communications outreach, and effectiveness.

After reworking the taxonomy, we were poised for implementation. Unlike many of our funding colleagues, we decided that results should not be anonymous. We expected investees to use the McKinsey-based assessment grid to develop their annual work plans; we also expected them to share their results with us. This is because SVP's philosophy is to meet an organization where they are and work with them for three to five years on capacity building. To tailor our extensive capacity-building support, we need to understand the unique strengths, weaknesses, and priorities of our investees. Conversely, for investees to effectively tap SVP for support, candor is essential. We hoped that our investees would recognize this philosophy, thereby reducing the likelihood that they would "inflate" their scores.

Outcomes

After two consecutive years of using the grid, it's hard to imagine that we ever built capacity effectively without the tool. The assessment process has accelerated understanding of investees' needs, and deepened their understanding of themselves. It's proven to be an essential starting point for discussion and planning, especially among staff and board members who might not otherwise be engaged in conversations about capacity building. As one investee noted, "The structure provided by the capacity assessment tool is very powerful. It's a well-distilled template for thinking about how you plan all aspects of your organization."

The challenge ahead is to determine if the McKinsey-based assessment instrument lives up to our long-term aspirations to measure change over time and identify the areas where SVP has the biggest impact. We need a few more years of data to draw these conclusions. Another outstanding question is whether the tool maintains its usefulness to investees over time. We suspect that the most engaging and rigorous use of the tool will happen in its initial use. With this in mind, we intend to ask investees to review the results and prioritization every other year rather than reuse the tool from scratch on an annual basis. Finally, now that we've been using the tool for two years, we can readily identify the ways in which it might be strengthened, primarily by adding additional questions. These modifications might take the form of a more expansive version of the tool, or simply the creation of a compendium to beef up specific areas. In considering a new version of the tool, we'll be forced to weigh the merits of increasing its usefulness and breadth, while maintaining manageability to investees and consistency of our own systems and processes.

A copy of SVP Seattle's version of the capacity assessment tool can be found on the CD accompanying this book and at http://www.svpseattle.org/key_documents.

CHAPTER 2

*Cap*Map®: Producing Breakthrough Capacity

by Maria Gutierrez and Daraus Mirza, Local Initiatives Support Corporation

Imagine climbing to the mountaintop, only to discover that beyond the cloud cover lies an uncharted and unknown territory—and the equipment you have is not up to the job! After years of innovating and succeeding with organizational assessments, performance standards, best practices, operating support, outcomes target planning, and a laundry list of other approaches, the Local Initiatives Support Corporation (LISC) had received considerable acclaim for helping our partner organizations grow and thrive. But the ground we now surveyed fell short of what we knew it could be. Too many organizations were overwhelmed by all the advice on what they "could" or "should" be, and were running at full steam just to sustain what they were already doing. Thinly structured and staffed, they frequently had little or no time to devote to the myriad of suggested capacity-building activities. As a result, many of them weren't "lean and mean"—they were frail and fragile! After consulting our peer organizations, it became clear that many saw LISC as the leading innovator in our field, and sympathetically advised that capacity building is simply a messy business. Yet, sensing that "good enough" thinking would never get us where we were committed to going, we went in search of a breakthrough.

Thankfully, we got one. How did it happen? Over the last four years, incorporating the vast experience and passion of our program staff, we have constructed and tested a model to define stages of organizational growth. We call the approach Capacity Mapping, and the tool, *Cap*Map. This is the *Cap*Map story.

The Road to *Cap*Map®

Building community development corporations (CDCs) into powerful change agents has been LISC's core business since our founding almost twenty-five years ago. Through our thirty-eight local program sites, we provide CDCs annually with direct project investment of approximately $500 million and more than $35 million in capacity-building grants and operating support. LISC has invested a wide range of resources in more than 2,400 not-for-profit CDCs that are physically and economically transforming their communities. The result: the millions of dollars in real estate assets that they now steward, the hundreds of thousands of housing units they have built, and the increasing vibrancy and economic viability of the neighborhoods where they live and work.

LISC uses a unique locally based model. Program staff living and working in cities across the country develop deep relationships with our partner CDCs. All program sites offer substantial capacity-building assistance to their CDCs. In many sites, LISC has established and manages funding collaboratives that pool the resources of local funders and channel them to partner CDCs. These collaboratives have led to profound capacity gains and neighborhood improvements.

Chapter Overview

Frustrated with its inability to find even a common language for talking about capacity, LISC program staff in 2000–2002 began constructing and testing a model to define stages of organizational growth. The approach is called Capacity Mapping, and the tool, *Cap*Map. This chapter will explain

- The road to *Cap*Map: A historical perspective on the need for a tool
- The birth and development of *Cap*Map: The people who worked on, and ideas that became part of, the tool

- The benefits of *Cap*Map: New opportunities and new directions
- Using *Cap*Map: An overview of the process
- Reactions to *Cap*Map from CDCs and LISC field offices
- What's next? The potential for taking *Cap*Map industrywide

---

While all LISC offices concern themselves with the organizational development of partner CDCs, many of our program sites have dedicated and professionally trained organizational development (OD) specialists on staff who design and manage all local capacity-building programming. These field-based practitioners constantly experiment with new ways to develop and support our CDC partners. They build relationships with their partner CDCs, choreograph the delivery of technical and financial resources, and help find solutions to difficult challenges. Because LISC OD practitioners work in the community, they understand the opportunities, threats, and pressures each CDC faces, and they are alert for early signs of trouble in the organization. They are supported in their work by LISC's Organizational Development Initiative (ODI), a national in-house management consulting, technical assistance, and training division.

LISC has a history of and reputation for state-of-the-art capacity building. We pioneered groundbreaking funding collaboratives. Researchers from around the world have studied our approaches and consulted with us on how they could adapt our models. We were at the cutting edge of outcomes measurement and emerging training trends in areas such as asset management. And we were an early adopter of now-common adult learning methods, with focus on dialogue, respect for the learner, and learning-by-doing.

In spring 2000, more than thirty of LISC's OD program staff met in Houston to discuss the current state of capacity building in our organization and in the community development industry more generally. We found that we shared frustrations in measuring the effectiveness of our efforts. As early pioneers in using the Outcomes Framework, a model for targeting higher organizational performance, many of our program staff were *already* firmly committed to a results-focused approach. But staff (and funders) wanted more. An increasing demand for performance standards, program evaluation, and community impact measures, and an overall trend toward more rigorous, data-based organizational development strategies showed a connection between *practice* and *results*.

Besides these trends, we were frustrated. We *knew* we had a vast amount of practical and tacit knowledge. Although we had embraced many cutting-edge, knowledge-sharing techniques, we sensed we were missing opportunities—perhaps even repeating mistakes—because we were not able to leverage all that we knew we knew among our dispersed programs or within the field. Some key questions arose:

- What are the most effective strategies for helping organizations grow?

- How could we most efficiently evaluate an organization's current capacity and its readiness for change?

- How could we figure out a CDC's best "next steps" in building capacity?

- How could we transfer information efficiently about which interventions worked, and which didn't?

These questions helped us realize that we lacked a common language for talking about capacity. Many professions have their own unique terms and units of measurement. Tailors have bolts, skeins, and yards; sailors have knots; winemakers have magnums; and jewelers have their carats. We needed to document the specific attributes of "high-performing" organizations. We needed a common language to describe the stages of organizational growth so that we could intervene appropriately and effectively with CDCs across the country—all at different stages in their development.

Deeper than language, we needed to agree on what constituted "capacity." "Capacity is in the eyes of the beholder," said one practitioner. One OD professional's "great" organization was another's mediocre one. Yet another said, "What's capacity? We know it, when we see it. The only problem is that, until we see them start to produce more, we're not sure they're on the right road. There's no intermediate measures or tests we can use to confirm they are flying right."

A good map is hard to find

We looked to academic models for capacity, but our practitioners found that academic models of organizational development did not work for real-world CDCs. Models that segmented organizations into static categories based on age missed the dynamic nature of community organizations where capacity can be significantly altered by the departure of one key staff person. Labels such as "nascent," "mature," and "emerging," are helpful in broad academic discourse, but can't help one make specific capacity-building investment decisions.

We also looked to the old-school-style assessments. Over the years, organizational assessments had become a standard feature of our capacity-building work. But we began to see that they created many problems of their own:

- Many assessments suffered from the "If all you have is a hammer, every problem looks like a nail" syndrome

- Reports were skewed toward the consultant's (or consulting team's) particular areas of expertise

- Reports took weeks or months to produce, leaving the client organizations in a state of limbo

- "Best practices" approaches detailed every organizational deficiency and had endless recommendations that read like long to-do lists that failed to prioritize the real critical issues

- Sometimes CDCs rejected the findings and recommendations of the consultant assessors, charging that they were biased, overly judgmental, or simply inappropriate for their stage of development

- The process was expensive, leaving little money leftover to implement any recommendations

- The net impact too often was to deflate the CDC's morale and sap their energy, leaving leaders defensive, insecure, and not motivated to change

- They were inconsistent and almost impossible to use for ongoing evaluation of our capacity-building work or to effectively benchmark organizations, either to themselves over time or to others

These models and assessment approaches failed at answering some of the most practical, pressing questions. Where should we target grant dollars and technical assistance? What precise new capacities will help a CDC achieve higher levels of performance? How do we *measure* organizational capacity? What are *indicators* of capacity in action? What is the *test* of capacity? How do we evaluate capacity in a way that charts a trajectory for *growth*? We needed to find a way to capture real time information about an organization's current capacity, both strengths and challenges, and in enough detail to be "actionable" by both our staff and the CDC's own leadership.

One thing we all agreed on was that we needed a new way of evaluating the current baseline capacity, and then we needed a shared method for measuring the progress improvements.

Nationally, in LISC's Organizational Development Initiative, we observed that many organizations we worked with seemed to need basic, remedial assistance. We wanted to develop standardized technical assistance programs in key operational areas such as financial management or asset management. These programs would move organizations through a series of carefully constructed developmental interventions to achieve consistent, competent levels of performance in each operational area. Each program would be "stepped" so that participants achieved a basic competency before moving on to more sophisticated ones.

This idea quickly morphed into a challenge and a group project: Could we articulate a developmental maturity model for CDC growth, one that stated the critical gates most organizations passed through as they became more sophisticated and capable? We weren't sure, but we were excited by the possibilities. Every LISC OD specialist in the room had committed, in addition to their local "day" jobs, to work on an initiative that would end up being the largest collaborative project development effort ever launched at LISC.

Birth and Development of *Cap*Map®

From 2000–2002, teams of LISC OD program officers worked on shaping the two elements that would eventually become *Cap*Map. First, it provides a developmental growth model that allows us to diagnose organizational maturity and consistently measure capacity gains over time. Second, it helps us develop *capacity mapping,* a process of engagement and collaboration that honors the experience of leaders in the field and brings to them the powerful knowledge of their peers.

Developed by more than fifty LISC OD practitioners, with input from numerous experts in the field, *Cap*Map was designed *by* LISC staff *for* LISC staff to make our collective efforts at CDC capacity building more informed, targeted, and more effective. *Cap*Map assists our program staff in evaluating the current capacity of an organization, working with a CDC to determine a path for growth, and measuring achievement along the way.

By providing good capacity intelligence appropriate to an organization's current maturity, *Cap*Map helps LISC program staff identify the most important and immediate needs so we can target capacity-building resources for maximum impact. Using *Cap*Map, LISC staff build organizational relationships, identify specific areas of long-term organizational growth, achieve organizational support for change, plan the use of resources more effectively, and evaluate the impact of their collective capacity-building efforts. Both the tool and the process are equally important components of LISC's holistic approach to capacity building.

Both the tool and the process are equally important components of LISC's holistic approach to capacity building.

A number of guiding principles influenced *Cap*Map's development, and provided the underpinning for the process. Many of them are based on years of lessons learned. They also resolve many of the problems we found in the academic and practitioner-based assessment approaches noted above:

- It is possible and necessary for LISC to capture the expert systems, experience, and tacit learning of our long-tenured field staff in order to transfer knowledge most effectively throughout the company and to be the best we can possibly be at organization building.

- The vast majority of organizations pass through certain shared milestones as they become increasingly more sophisticated in a capacity area, and it is possible to identify these stages of growth.

- No *inherent* inadequacy is suggested by the attainment of any particular stage. Many assessment systems rely on so-called best practices, with each deviation an organization demonstrates representing a "failing." *Cap*Map resists a value-laden approach. It attempts to describe how CDCs really grow, based upon our collective experience. *Cap*Map recognizes that organizations, like people, can be masterful in one area, and yet weak in another, despite organizational longevity.

- Organizational capacity *is* as organizational capacity *does*. Organizations at higher stages of capacity are able to "do" things that organizations at lower stages cannot. Thus, we attempt to describe these "action-oriented" competencies in measurable and verifiable terms. *Cap*Map is outcomes oriented.

• Expert systems get expert results. *Cap*Map looks to the *underlying organizational systems* that result in production. These systems ensure organizational stability and ongoing competency beyond the current circumstances. While production may be the ultimate goal, operating systems are the vehicle for reaching that goal and then hitting it again and again. A model that analyzes only performance outputs can fail to reflect significant organizational challenges and weaknesses that will affect long-term effectiveness.

• Engaging an organization's leadership in a collaborative discovery process that is transparent and obvious empowers them as actors, not subjects, in their own organizational development. Capacity mapping is not an end in itself. It is a shared effort that builds continuously renewable energy for change. *A capacity map is the beginning, not the end, of a change project.*

*Cap*Map®: A diagnostic instrument

*Cap*Map is a developmental growth model that distinguishes progressive stages of competency in nine key areas of organizational activity that we believe are crucial for success. These key areas are:

• Board governance

• Community connections

• Executive leadership

• Financial management

• Fund development

• Human resources and staff development

• Management information systems (MIS)

• Real estate asset management

• Real estate development

By providing verifiable measures about operational capacity within each of these key areas, *Cap*Map complements traditional analytical techniques such as ratio analysis and key performance indicators. *Cap*Map provides deeper insight into the systems that are producing results. Most important, *Cap*Map looks at the key characteristics of "capacity in action"—what organizations with higher stages of capacity *can do* that organizations at lower stages simply cannot. By reflecting capacity in action versus capacity at rest (that is, proof that the organization *utilizes* the resources and systems it has to further its mission), *Cap*Map helps to focus on the current state of an organization and its ability to produce long-term results.

Ten competency stages within each key area module form the basis of a capacity-building map for an organization. After identifying where an organization currently is, the module then indicates the critical milestone an organization should achieve on its unique path of growth. Each *Cap*Map module consists of ten stages, or steps. Each stage consists of the following components:

- A statement of that stage's **critical competencies**

- A corresponding list of **verifications** that tell whether or not the competency exists at that time

- A set of activities referred to as **indicators**—experiences that often exist in an organization performing at that competency stage

- A list of suggestions called **capacity builders** that point an organization toward experiences that define the next competency stage

Critical competencies

Staff teams were assigned a key area and were asked to develop the growth module: ten *progressive* stages of competency that signify progressive organizational capacity. These we call *critical competencies*. This task is deceptively simple to state, but very difficult to accomplish. Staff had to sift through mountains of experiential data to identify the key milestones of organizational capacity. Fine-tuning the stages required looking at organizational growth along a developmental continuum.

We repeatedly encouraged the teams to step back, examine their career experiences, and try to pinpoint the crucial but nuanced changes organizations go through. What can they do that is unique as they become increasingly sophisticated? was a question we continually asked ourselves. What important characteristics and abilities truly distinguish one organization from another that has not yet reached that same level of ability? What can they do, that another cannot? And why?

Finally, we challenged each team to articulate the *critical* competency for each stage. Drawing on the human development model as an analogy, we sought to define similar organizational tipping points. For instance, a toddler develops many new skills during the course of this stage: elementary cognizant abilities, language, and independent movement. But the defining characteristic is that they walk or "toddle." Identifying the critical competencies for organizations was part of the effort to pare down our knowledge base to a manageable but elegant simplicity. Below are a few examples of critical competencies from the Financial Management *Cap*Map module:

- Stage Three: CDC protects its assets through standardized internal controls

- Stage Four: CDC financial statements are timely, accurate, and accrual based

- Stage Seven: CDC analyzes historical data and utilizes analysis in management decision-making

One of the greatest challenges throughout this process was the temptation to describe a best practice or "best-in-class behavior" too early in the developmental scale. We had to remind ourselves continually of our commitment to describe not what we would have *liked* to see in some best-of-all-possible-world theoretic model, but rather what, in fact, we *were* seeing as we worked with organizations over time. The exercise demanded that we resist our natural tendency to simply identify the best practice in every instance and instead capture the markers of the natural development of organizations. We continually stressed the need to focus on descriptions of what we were really seeing out there in the field, not what we thought we should be seeing.

Verifications

Verification is the core of our process and defines *Cap*Map's true value. *Verifications* are simple yes-or-no questions, generally three or four per competency stage, and are designed to be fairly easy to administer. Some questions require the user to examine documents or files, and some allow the organization to self-report on practices or systems. Because we proscribed a limit on the number of verifications any stage would have, and decided that all questions should be answered yes in order to attain that stage, the questions had to reflect a truly critical aspect of the overall competency. Here are a few examples of verifications from the Financial Management *Cap*Map module:

- Are the bank statements reconciled by a person who does not write or sign checks?
- Is the CDC able to produce financial reports within 15 days of the close of the month?
- Does CDC have an indirect cost allocation system?
- Have the unrestricted net assets increased over the last three years?

Unlike some diagnostic processes, we do not expect *Cap*Map to test or prove capacity beyond all doubt. We settled for reasonable, if not definitive, information about an organization's current maturity. However, we did vote for clear measurability and cut-and-dried answers, with little space for judgment calls. This decision led to the often painstaking process of creating rigorous verifications that captured organizational complexity in a few words. Identifying the correct tests and verifications was almost as difficult as defining the critical competencies.

From the beginning, we stressed the need to keep verifications simple, speedy, and constructed in a way to avoid confusing the assessed organization. Thus, organizations either pass the verification or they don't; they either have the competency or they don't. As a tool to be utilized by our staff, who come to the work from diverse backgrounds, experiences and expertise, *Cap*Map is easy to use and provides the maximum amount of information in the minimum amount of time. In addition, *Cap*Map is both a tool and a process that rejects an "audit" mentality, characterized by distance and distrust that is antithetical to our goals of collaboration and partnership. Finally, the consistency of the verifications enables more people to successfully administer the modules while keeping our data consistent.

Indicators

If the answers to the verification questions yield mixed results or the user wants further clarification, each competency stage also includes a list of indicators. *Indicators* are activities that are often performed in organizations that have demonstrated the competency stage and help "indicate" the presence of the competency. Indicators detail specific systems, procedures, and practices that organizations that have attained a particular stage commonly demonstrate. While the presence of any individual indicator, in and of itself, does not conclusively prove that a competency has been reached, together they allow the *Cap*Map users to accumulate a preponderance of evidence based upon the activities the organization engages in. More important, the indicators give an organization specific insight into what they need to do differently in order to attain the competency. Here are a few examples also from the Financial Management *Cap*Map module:

- Board minutes reflect discussion and adoption of financial policies and procedures

- CDC external financial statements conform with current standards (GAAP and FASB)

- Key financial ratios are tracked and reviewed quarterly

- CDC analyzes monthly cash flow

The teams generally found the creation of indicators to be easier during the development of *Cap*Map. Conditioned to look for signs of organizational competence, they were able to quickly detail long lists of activities and work practices associated with any particular competency.

Capacity builders

Capacity builders (labeled *Cap*Builders in the tool) are resources, activities, interventions, and other strategies that an organization can use to move to the next stage of competency. They guide LISC program staff in working with CDC staff and board members to identify capacity-building strategies. Recommended strategies may include a variety of technical assistance options, tools, and software; consultant services; networking opportunities; recommended readings; and education or training available to strengthen staff skills.

The *Cap*Builder section is comprehensive but by no means complete. It invites every user to plumb his or her experience and creativity to come up with additional ideas. Along with resource suggestions, the *Cap*Builder section often makes specific recommendations for operational practice or procedure improvements. Here are some examples of *Cap*Builders from the Financial Management *Cap*Map module:

- Schedule an annual financial audit and present the findings, including a management letter, to the board of directors

- Consolidate all financial management policies and procedures in a manual

- Develop internal and external financial benchmarks to serve as a basis for evaluating performance

- Review cost allocation formulas with accountant/consultant to make sure they accurately reflect program expenses

Piloting and refinement

The design of *Cap*Map and the content of this unique tool reflect the recommendations and contributions of not only LISC staff, but numerous practitioners working in the field for and with CDCs. We partnered with many of our CDCs early in the development of *Cap*Map in order to solicit feedback from their staff and board members about the value and utility of the tool. As a prototype of each module was developed, we piloted it extensively with CDCs across the country. We used the feedback we gained from both the organizations being mapped and LISC staff members to refine the instrument and the process we were recommending. This feedback frequently revealed areas where we needed to do a better job in training our own staff to execute the approach. After developing a working set of modules, we invited comment on the content and proposed processes from outside consultants and specialists in specific capacity areas.

During this period, LISC staff continued to introduce *Cap*Map to our partner CDCs across LISC sites, soliciting both formal and informal responses to the process and approach. National ODI staff trained local staff and local advisory committees on capacity mapping through presentations, coaching sessions, and workshops. As we refined *Cap*Map, we explored, validated, and sometimes discarded theories we had developed over the years about how to work best with organizations. We also learned significant lessons about how to communicate with our partners, and how to prepare and train our staff to execute the capacity-mapping approach.

Thus ends the story of the drivers for and development of *Cap*Map. Next we'll look at it benefits and use.

Benefits of *Cap*Map®

*Cap*Map is helping LISC staff and our partner CDCs to

- *Determine the competencies that are needed to achieve an organization's vision. Cap*Map is based on the belief that expert results are produced by expert systems. The internal structures, procedures, and administration of an organization determine its capacity to mobilize resources and advance its mission. The more expert—or competent—an organization is in key areas, the more it will be able to achieve. *Cap*Map outlines progressive stages of competency and describes what most organizations at the varying stages are able to produce and act on. This helps an organization to determine what stage of competency it wants to achieve to produce the results it envisions.

- *Identify organizational priorities and next steps.* Once an organization clearly understands where it *is* and where *it wants to be, Cap*Map can help point the way to where it needs to go *next.* By identifying progressive stages of competency, *Cap*Map outlines the critical gates that an organization should be passing through as its capacity continues to grow. Unlike assessments, which can sometimes be overwhelming and leave the CDC with a lengthy list of items for improvement, *Cap*Map suggests a priority and path for growth. Organizations are able to see how they might progress toward their goals, and then work with LISC to identify how to start moving from where they are toward where they are going. This enables LISC to target capacity-building funds to the area most needed to move an organization from one stage of competency to the next.

• *Educate and enroll the entire organization in the process of capacity building.* Different people with different roles in the same organization often have a different understanding of what is needed for growth. Some may not be aware that much is needed at all. *Cap*Map helps an organization reach a common understanding of current capacity and chart a path for organizational growth. A CDC can use the capacity-mapping process to collectively identify capacity needs and communicate the benefits of capacity building across the organization. Enrolling the entire organization in a change process is a critical component of success, and helps to ensure that capacity-building efforts will "take" in the organization.

• *Measure the success of capacity-building efforts and verify the results of interventions.* Using *Cap*Map over time provides a measure of organizational growth and can confirm that capacity-building efforts are yielding results. Higher levels of competency are the ultimate desired impact of trainings or targeted interventions. *Cap*Map can serve as a means for quantifying an organization's growth, thereby enabling LISC to realistically verify the impact and success of our efforts. In addition to providing information that can increase LISC's own effectiveness, this focus on concrete results also simplifies reporting to funders for both LISC and the CDC.

• *Establish trends and allow for greater targeting of programs within a site.* When *Cap*Map is conducted for CDCs within the same region, a capacity map of the industry in that geographic area emerges. Program staff can then identify areas of need and create programs and trainings targeted toward those areas. A LISC office has much better advance knowledge of what specific kinds of trainings will be most useful to local CDCs, as well as how basic or advanced the training content should be to be useful to participants. Having a broader sense of regional capacity needs, as well as the history and outcomes of past capacity-building strategies, can also help LISC to identify the types of interventions that would be most likely to yield the desired results.

• *Assist in improved management of consultants.* Having a baseline of capacity enables a CDC, and its funders, to identify areas that would benefit from technical assistance or other consulting services. *Cap*Map's emphasis on capacity-building strategies assists CDCs in providing a clear vision of what they want the consultant to accomplish, and what the organization should accomplish as a result of the consultation. This concentration on results also allows LISC to better assess whether the consultant and the organization have ultimately been successful in creating and sustaining organizational change.

The Value of a Good Map

A good map helps locate you in the universe. It makes no value judgment about whether it is more desirable to go to Cleveland or Detroit; it lays out the options, but does not insist upon where, or even whether, one must travel. Such decisions are left to the whims, desires, and agenda of each traveler. But what it does do is provide a sense of the road ahead, how long the trip may take, any shortcuts that might be possible, key landmarks along the way that indicate you are on the right path, a sense of the obstacles that may be encountered, and whether you are on the scenic route.

A good map allows the new traveler to benefit from the experience of others who have gone before and, hopefully, to navigate with greater ease because of earlier hard-won lessons. A good map is a comfort, providing confidence to its user—whatever the road may bring, you won't be navigating blind: you've got a resource you can always refer to. In a strange new place, it helps a user acclimate faster and understand the broader landscape in a way that is not possible from the vantage point of any individual road, no matter how "right" the road may turn out to be.

Our goal with *Cap*Map was to create such a map—one that was accurate, yet allowed each CDC to place itself in the universe and set its sites on the place it wished to travel. Some organizations take the fast route, and some take the scenic route. The important thing is that all organizations using the map know where they are and where they're going.

Using *Cap*Map®: An Overview

Preparing to map

*Cap*Map is a time-efficient modularized tool that provides significant diagnostic flexibility to our staff. At many LISC sites, *Cap*Map is a core component of a larger program design. In these cases, LISC typically prescribes the modules that will be used with all organizations participating in a given capacity-building program or operating support collaborative. We may require participating organizations to complete some or all of the modules in order to be considered for further funding. In other cases, local programs have opted to allow CDC leadership to participate in selecting the modules they want to use. In still other cases, *Cap*Map is delivered on an as-needed basis where LISC program staff draw on their deep knowledge of the organization and what they perceive as its immediate needs or challenge areas. They then select one or a combination of the modules to be used. Some offices have created a *Cap*Map rollout process that spans several years, with all organizations in the site conducting two to three maps a year. In these cases, LISC often ties its follow-up resource investments to the same areas mapped, and creates extensive programs to support growth in these capacities. Frequently, program staff have preferred to start mapping in areas of core business competence: the Board Development, Real Estate Development, and Financial Management modules. From there, they customize the mix of *Cap*Map modules based on their findings, and an organization's interests.

To ensure that every part of our process reflects our deep respect for an organization's knowledge and experience, program staff are strongly encouraged to provide the CDC's leadership with a copy of the module ahead of time. A CDC version does not include the CapBuilder column or instructions in the verification column that are intended only for LISC staff. While LISC staff share and discuss capacity-building strategies with the CDC, the absence of the CapBuilder column allows LISC to keep the focus on establishing an accurate baseline *before* discussing specific intervention options.

In some cases, staff decide not to send the CDC an advance copy of the module. These staff choose to share a module only onsite during the visit to avoid having the CDC staff and board predetermine their competency stage or rehearse answers. The decision to share or not to share should be based on the program staff's relationship with the CDC and knowledge of the organization's institutional honesty. We generally discourage the withholding of the module because we believe that there is so much to be gained by sharing it. Regardless of the decision to share or not to share the modules in advance, we always send a list of the documents CDCs need to compile prior to the visit.

Advance communications

LISC OD practitioners frequently report that extensive communication with their CDCs prior to the mapping has helped the process run much more smoothly. Most have also found these conversations helped LISC forge a more open and productive partnership with the CDC. Therefore, LISC staff generally spend a great deal of time introducing *Cap*Map to our partner CDCs, answering questions and concerns before scheduling any visits.

When we initially rollout *Cap*Map in a site, the local program will often host a breakfast or lunch presentation to introduce *Cap*Map to all the groups, inviting board members, executive directors, and other staff as well as local stakeholder partners to learn about the capacity-mapping process. National ODI staff frequently present some portion of the program, sharing the genesis of the approach as well as information about the use of *Cap*Map at other program sites. Participants are generally excited by the prospect of being able to benchmark themselves against their peers around the country, and the opportunity to access specific information about how other organizations have achieved higher levels of capacity. In many presentations, we share the results from mapping engagements in other areas, continually affirming the value of organizational knowledge-sharing. After the group presentation, local LISC staff will typically follow up with each individual organization's leadership to further discuss the process and its goals.

Once an organization has committed to the process, a preinterview letter is sent describing how to prepare for capacity mapping and what the CDC should expect during the interview visit. It also provides a written explanation of the process for CDC representatives who may not have attended the presentation or introductory meeting. In the letter, we invite the executive director to identify the appropriate staff members who should be interviewed—they usually select the staff members who oversee the functions for the areas being mapped. For example, because the aim of this visit is to talk to the person who can most efficiently tell us about the activities of the specific operational area that is being mapped, we would want to talk to the chief financial officer or bookkeeper for the financial management capacity mapping. Along with the letter we generally provide the *Cap*Map modules. This gives the CDC advance knowledge of the topics to be discussed and an opportunity to prepare relevant information.

Transparent process

LISC program staff attempt to make the process obvious and transparent. Part of the discomfort organizations feel about being assessed is the mystery and obscurity that often surrounds much of the experience. They usually do not get to choose the assessor, and may have no knowledge of the assessor's qualifications. They frequently do not understand the basis or context for many of the lines of questioning or the need for requested documents. They may not understand why the diagnostic is even needed in the first place, let alone trust the reasons given by the funders. With little control over a process that infantilizes them, it should not be surprising if they reject the assessor's recommendations and findings or fail to recognize themselves in the consultant's final report.

Because *CapMap* specifically details the collective knowledge of their peers, *LISC staff do not need to be expert in every capacity area to use those particular modules effectively.* However, they do need to be able to clarify the questions they are asking and understand the answers they receive, ask appropriate follow up questions and review any necessary documentation. In some cases, they may choose to invite other staff members from their offices who may have a broader knowledge of the subject matter to participate in mappings outside their core competence areas.

During the visit

Once LISC staff arrive at the CDC office for interviews, our goal is to continue to build positive energy and enthusiasm for change. We place a high value on communication and relationship building. To begin, we again communicate to each interviewee the goals for the mapping, the benefits of accessing knowledge about the organizational development of peers, and the opportunity to benchmark their own performance. We continually strive to distinguish this process from other assessment experiences that they may have had. For instance, unlike most assessors, our staff do not need to spend much time establishing their own credibility as an expert. In fact, we have found that it is much more effective for them to forgo the power differential associated with expert status and instead attempt to close the distance between the assessor and the assessed. This is often accomplished by conveying to the organization's staff the sense that as a team, they hope to work collaboratively through this national model together, discovering what might be useful for their particular needs. The value of the model lies in its intellectual capital—the articulation of the developmental path of so many other community development organizations—not in the individual knowledge base of any one LISC program officer.

In addition, we affirm our commitment to partnership and collaborative discovery, and attempt to establish a friendly, conversational tone throughout the interviews. As we strive to help a CDC identify its current capacity in the context of what is possible, we engage in a dialogue that is anything but an audit-like cross-examination. Throughout the interviews, which typically take only two to three hours per module, our goal is to enroll CDC staff fully in the discovery process, helping to build their capacity for self-reflection in an atmosphere of safety and trust. Before, during, and at the end of the interviews we make it clear to the grantees and interviewees that all conversations in the mapping process are confidential. We treat them as equal partners through our behavior, attitude, and approach. LISC staff members take specific steps to make the interview experience an honest and open exchange of ideas. At the end of the process, we hope participants report that they have a deeper understanding of what kinds of systems are being utilized in the day-to-day operation and where there may be room for growth, and that they are motivated and inspired enough by what others have done before them that they choose to invest their resources to create positive change.

Mapping is only the beginning

We encourage staff to stay in inquiry mode throughout the interview, and to resist a rush to judgment about which stage an organization has attained until they have had time to reflect quietly on all the data they gathered. As they work through the questions with the CDC, it should be fairly obvious to all participants which stages were or were not attained. However, in some cases, the answers are not so clear, and coming to a reasonable determination may require reflection and additional review. For this reason, LISC staff typically share their observations at a follow-up meeting a week or two later, where they provide a simple report detailing the results of each verification by stage. Unlike typical final assessment reports that can be twenty, thirty, or forty pages filled with narrative, *Cap*Map results are conveyed through a simple template. It shows specifically which systems and processes are currently in place and practiced, and where there may be gaps or room for improvement.

The reports also contain concise LISC staff notes, remarks, and observations along with a *short* list of recommended activities that will help the CDC achieve the next capacity stage along the *Cap*Map continuum. The goal is brevity and focus! This face-to-face report may take place with CDC leadership including board members or with all staff involved in the mapping process. It may include a PowerPoint presentation summarizing the content of the individual maps. CDC staff and board members are invited to clarify any misunderstandings, ask any questions, and provide us with feedback on the process. Frequently, these reports have already been vetted with the executive director of the CDC to ensure accuracy. If the mapping has gone well, there should be few surprises for the CDC staff who participated in the process. They should clearly recognize the reflection of themselves in the organizational mirror *Cap*Map holds up. This follow-up meeting also provides an opportunity for us to learn which areas of capacity the organization is energized to work on, and thus to target the kind of supports we might offer them.

Timely follow-up is a key part of a successful mapping process. Mapping is only the first step in a comprehensive organizational approach that includes target planning, intervention and resource application, and remapping and evaluation. To capitalize fully on the momentum and energy that *Cap*Map can generate, the organization that is mapped needs to process and understand the findings quickly and then move into growth planning and implementation phases.

Following a mapping, LISC staff work with the CDC to determine where it wants to go and how to get there. The information gathered through the capacity-mapping process enables a CDC and LISC to map out a game plan. In many sites, organizations are asked to develop outcomes-based target plans that then form the basis for LISC operating support or capacity-building investment. These target plans constitute a form of contract between an organization's leadership and the LISC office as investors. These plans do not need to address every mapped area, but there is usually an expectation that a group commit to improving in at least one critical competency area. The area they select to work on and make a part of their work plan is sometimes the subject of negotiation between the organization and LISC staff, but generally there is a high degree of agreement on what capacity areas are important enough to merit the next investment.

*Cap*Map empowers an organization's leadership because they can see for themselves what different capacity levels look like—not just on paper but in terms of what an organization is able to produce and act on. CDC leadership is barraged daily by intelligence on best practices; what frequently baffles them is how to decide among competing great ideas. One of *Cap*Map's true contributions to the field is that it helps these primary players sort through the plethora of worthwhile options and identify the "next-best" capacity for their particular organization to invest its precious time and energy in building. Working together, CDC leadership and LISC staff can consult the *Cap*Builder suggested approaches: suitable trainings for individual staff, technical assistance ideas for systems development, grantmaking strategies, suggested hardware or software, and so forth. *Cap*Map aims to demystify organizational development and open a dialogue that enrolls all parties in discussing and plotting the best investment of scarce time, technical assistance, or training resources.

After capacity mapping and identifying opportunities for growth, LISC staff and the organization's management team (usually the executive director and/or board members) develop strategies. Each strategy contains details with specific targets and goals to be achieved by the organization within a defined period of time. The time period the organization plans for the execution of these strategies is typically nine months to a year. These targets are usually owned by various individuals within the organization. Everyone involved works toward accomplishing the goals agreed upon, and often specific funding is connected to many of the targets. LISC staff members bring in resources or allocate funds for interventions, and when necessary, the CDC approaches other funders or entities for support in achieving the targets. Although specific internal capacity gains are usually a required deliverable for much of our operating support or capacity-building programs, outcome target plans almost always include production and other performance goals for the organization as well.

It is important to note that many of the activities that *Cap*Map proposes for increasing capacity are not necessarily expensive or do not even require financial support to implement. For example, a recommendation for increasing board capacity may be to have board meetings at least quarterly with a quorum present, or adopt a conflict of interest policy, which will help ensure that the governing body complies with legal and ethical requirements of the nonprofit. An example within the human resources and staff development capacity areas would be that the organization adopts templates for commonly used personnel forms, such as vacation request, timesheets, sick leave, and personal leave so that records are organized, up-to-date, and useful to the management of the CDC.

Other recommended activities may require different levels of investment. Development of a comprehensive multiyear strategic plan may cost an organization a considerable amount of time and resources. A CDC may need to upgrade or purchase new financial accounting software to produce timely and accurate financial statements so leadership can monitor the financial performance of individual programs and the organization as a whole in an efficient manner.

Typically, the executive director and the staff of a CDC work with LISC to decide how to address the agreed-on interventions. Grantees at many LISC sites have long histories of using the outcomes framework as the way to create targets, develop milestones, and measure results for reporting. Following the same method, CDCs are encouraged to develop step-by-step action plans for each target, which are then used as a management tool throughout the implementation process. Typically, this approach provides managers with sufficient early information to correct their course when necessary. The CDCs generally report to LISC and other funders on their progress against each target on a regular basis, perhaps monthly or quarterly.

Achieving buy-in

Most community development corporations that LISC works with have been assessed by many different entities and often more than once—sometimes by funders, sometimes by the intermediaries, and other times by academic institutions. These experiences have often been organizationally painful and ineffective, leaving the leadership distrustful and wary. We realized early on that we needed to engage organizations in a manner that overcame their skepticism. From the beginning, we wanted to create a process that energized them and provided them with the tools to create the organizational change *they* wanted to achieve. Our goal is to ensure that these good intentions inform every element of the capacity-mapping process. The following precepts help us to achieve a high degree of buy-in from our partners.

1. *Communication is critical . . . right from the start.* We spend a good deal of time training our staff in how and what to communicate about *Cap*Map and the capacity-mapping process. Key elements to communicate include the following:

    - *Cap*Map is designed to reflect the path that most (but not all) of our highly competent organizations have traveled on their way to success—knowledge of their peers can be a powerful tool

    - *Cap*Map was designed with a great deal of input from our CDC partners and many longtime experts in the field

    - *Cap*Map provides organizations with information *they* will decide how to use

    - *Cap*Map does not judge whether organizations are competent enough— only whether they can do what they want to in the context of what they are trying to achieve

    - LISC is committed to partnering with organizations in a respectful and collaborative manner

2. *Be honest about expectations.* We encourage staff to be as open and honest about the process as they can and absolutely clear about program requirements for support.

3. *Respect the CDCs' knowledge.* No matter how much we think we know about them, the CDCs know more. They have the deepest knowledge and understanding of their organizations' issues. This knowledge is often the key to diagnosing the real causes of organizational impotence and finding the right leverage points to transform them. Our job is to get them to share it with us and to supplement it with our own.

4. *Be humble.* Our partners have the most noble role in the process. They are on the frontline every day. Whatever their past mistakes, whatever their failings, our job is to support them in achieving great things for their communities. Their success is our success, and if they fail, we have failed.

Internally, the process by which *Cap*Map was designed and tested generated organizational buy-in right from the start. The LISC staff who created *Cap*Map or contributed to its testing and rollout have a tremendous belief in its utility and a substantial ownership stake in its success. They have experienced first hand the level of diligence and effort, research and scholarship, field testing and rigor that has gone into its development. They are keenly aware of the possibilities this breakthrough opens up for us as an organization, and the power this model holds in the hands of an organization so well positioned to execute it. The approach has provided them with a vast storehouse of information that was previously unavailable or inaccessible. And most important, they are receiving positive feedback from our partner CDCs and achieving measurable, verifiable capacity-building results.

Last, local program staff know they will be supported by our national Organizational Development Initiative, which delivers training and ongoing coaching, along with new tools, templates, report formats, process improvements, and results analysis. Training for staff involved in capacity mapping is significant and includes use of the tool itself, how to establish collaborative relationships, interviewing techniques, diagnostic and consultative methods, and communication. And as new capacity-mapping needs emerge, the ODI strives to provide the research and development the field requires. This kind of ongoing support provides our staff with a significant level of confidence as they explore uncharted new frontiers.

There is an occupational hazard that is unavoidable: many organizations resist facing uncomfortable or difficult realities, even to the point of their own demise. Our challenge as change agents and cheerleaders is to find ways to help the organizations build a culture of self-reflection and a capacity for achieving continuous improvement. But unless the reasons for their resistance to change are surfaced in a constructive manner, we find organizations are usually unable to fully deal with the real issues, mired as they often are in excuses, denials, and justifications. Helping organizations identify and articulate the underlying causes of their resistance—often based in their fears of change, loss of control, or perceptions of vulnerability—is the first necessary step in assisting them.

Our entire mapping approach has been designed to create safety and openness, and to encourage honest organizational exploration. We model this ourselves. When introducing *Cap*Map, we stress that it was built largely to help us be more effective and accountable in supporting our partners. We share blind results from mapping engagements in other areas, complimenting the leadership and courage of these organizations. We convey our desire to serve. Especially important, we acknowledge that the assessment methods of the past have contributed to suspicions that funders all too often sit in judgment, distant and apart, with no real accountability for the success or failure of their capacity-building investments. When LISC program staff acknowledge accountability for achieving results in partnership with the organization, we begin to equalize the perceived power differential and place ourselves on a more equal footing with CDC leadership.

Reactions to *Cap*Map®

Encouraging stories are coming from CDCs all over the country crediting *Cap*Map with helping their organizations to grow. Most credit *Cap*Map with providing a clear understanding of the current ability of their existing systems, and helping them select and orchestrate a "just-in-time" path for improvement. Reports tell us that this growth has resulted in better internal structures, procedures, and administration. We've had excellent reports from LISC fields offices as well.

By using *Cap*Map across all their partner organizations, many LISC sites are able to identify areas of common weakness. Thus, they can develop comprehensive capacity-development programs to help many organizations. There are considerable cost savings when this is possible, and the ability to tailor technical assistance, training workshops, consultant services, and one-on-one coaching to specific and immediate needs. By adding more rigor and consistency to our diagnostic approach, we have also discovered numerous opportunities for leveraging knowledge more efficiently. For instance, information gleaned across multiple organizations has helped us set up appropriate practitioner support groups and other kinds of peer-to-peer learning opportunities with no breach in confidentiality. We are also better prepared to quietly broker mentoring and coaching relationships that support the industry and help build more capable leaders.

In Mid-South Delta LISC, for example, staff used the information gathered through the capacity-mapping process to identify a shared need for improved accounting systems in many of its CDCs. As a result, Mid-South Delta LISC developed an assistance program that provides CDCs with a customized software product, trains the staff in accounting systems and the use of the software, and provides ongoing support. Each CDC participating in the program receives a level of comprehensive technical assistance that would have been much more difficult and costly to deliver to the CDCs individually. And they have each other to call when one hits a snag—leveraging knowledge on their own!

Reactions from community development corporations

Opa-Locka CDC, Miami, FL

One of the first early and enthusiastic responses came from Willie Logan, president of Opa-Locka Community Development Corporation. When his high-performing organization was initially mapped in early 2002, he knew there were some financial management systems that were not supporting his information needs or those of the board of directors. He had an intuitive sense of what needed to be worked on next, based upon his many years of leadership experience, but wasn't entirely sure of some of the root causes of their reporting difficulties or the best next step for maximum impact and result. According to Logan, "the capacity-mapping process was an eye-opener. It led us to additional analysis of our financial management systems, purchase and implementation of more relevant software, and ultimately to better information." After the mapping was completed, the path for capacity growth at Opa-Locka was clear and, incidentally, validated many of Logan's gut instincts.

New Neighborhoods, Inc., Stamford, CT

Ross Burkhardt, president and chief executive officer of New Neighborhoods, Inc. (NNI), reports that the *Cap*Map process has been very helpful for his organization. The board and the staff are using the findings as a baseline for their strategic planning process. In fact, after the staff from the LISC Connecticut Statewide operation spent a day mapping four capacity areas at NNI, as well as interviewing and reviewing necessary systems that support the operation, Burkhardt and his staff were so energized by the process and the prospect of receiving valuable information about their organization that they invited LISC staff back for another day to perform mappings of additional competency areas. Although LISC originally focused on four areas of operation, it became clear to both partners (NNI and LISC) that the opportunity was too great to pass up.

Plymouth Housing Group, Seattle, WA

On the other side of the country, Teresa Donovan, deputy director of Plymouth Housing Group, said, "The [capacity-mapping] experience was a positive one for us. The process did not take very much time. It put us in touch with how accessible and current our information is, and it provided a guide for identifying information we should have. We found it [to be] a very valuable tool and we've used it to review what processes we can improve upon. It was fun to see what we were doing well and where we can improve." She added, "I found the interviewers very congenial and open. It was a wonderful opportunity to share experiences and ideas with individuals familiar with the nonprofit world. [It was a] very comfortable and nonthreatening review process."

Many leaders have agreed with Donovan's assessment of the process: they find it "comfortable," "open," and "nonthreatening." Some have even called it "fun." Often participants are quite surprised by the fluidity of this process and how much they learn just by participating in the interviews. Seeing excitement in staff and board members after the mapping has been a common experience for LISC staff across the country. Because *Cap*Map is modeled on the growth trajectory of numerous organizations LISC has had the honor of working with over the years, and focuses on what is present and possible as well as current strengths and what others have achieved before, it brings energy to organizations whether they are only beginning to realize their potential or have tried and failed to build their capacity many times in the past. The hope it creates is invigorating and helps to lift them out of whatever organizational malaise they may be experiencing.

Project Row Houses, Houston, TX

In Houston, where more than twenty groups have been mapped and remapped in the last few years, Deborah Grotfeldt, community development director of Project Row Houses (PRH), told us, "PRH is progressing in all of our community development initiatives thanks to full-time staff provided by the LISC Greater Houston Organizational Development Program and the capacity-mapping exercise, which has been tremendously helpful as we work toward a more efficient staff structure. The training opportunities suggested through *Cap*Map have also been tremendously helpful."

An interesting by-product of the mapping process observed by many of our LISC colleagues in the field is an improvement in internal communication in the mapped organizations. Staff and board members are reporting better communication and working relationships with more frequent collaboration after being mapped. Field staff have also pointed out that *Cap*Map recommendations are often strategies that need to be undertaken by both staff and board members, leading to more opportunities for collaborative work within the organizations.

Mid-South Delta OE Program

One of the most successful capacity-building initiatives at LISC was created in the Mid South Delta region. In late 2000, Glenn Nishimura, senior program director of Mid South Delta LISC, secured a generous grant from the Winthrop Rockefeller Foundation and started the Organizational Excellence Program. The program promised to focus on developing organizational capacity in CDCs that LISC works with in the Mississippi Delta. *Cap*Map was the core of this program and dictated the design and focus of the capacity-building efforts.

During summer 2001, local LISC staff members, supported by ODI staff, mapped twenty-five groups in four capacity areas across three Delta states—Arkansas, Louisiana, and Mississippi—and identified the baseline capacity for each of the groups. Using initial findings, LISC decided to put its primary focus on the financial management operation of these organizations, since all found it to be an area in dire need of attention. The Financial Management Project offered each CDC direct consultant time, choice of standard financial management software, and experts to install necessary programs as well as train CDC staff in operating it. Mid South Delta LISC also arranged additional technical assistance for staff and board members and convened small, focused group training workshops. In addition to financial management, LISC arranged direct support for the boards of directors to assist them in developing more effective governance capacity. This support took the form of training, executive coaching, board retreat opportunities, and strategic planning. Over the next two years, additional supports, both financial and technical, were given in real estate development and in several other capacity areas.

At the end of the third year, twenty-one groups were remapped to determine the progress they had made. The results were invigorating: twenty of the twenty-one groups still in business had increased their capacity by at least one stage in one or more capacity areas. For the first time, LISC was able to verify the return on capacity-building investments in a measurable way.

Many of the organizations were able to demonstrate dramatic growth in more than one capacity area. One such organization was Chicot Housing, which, in one year, increased its capacity in community connections by three stages and in financial management by four stages. Cathy Wilson, the LISC program officer administrating the Organizational Excellence Program in the Delta, wrote in a report to funders that "the beauty of *Cap*Map is that there is no subjectivity about that improved capacity." The findings "identify exactly what capacity has been built. . . . *Cap*Map gives [organizations] the tools to understand what they must do and helps them make the right moves." For investors in the Delta, it was clear that the capacity-mapping process was contributing to significant organizational growth. At the same time, it was providing investors with a means to demonstrate and verify the accomplishment of these organizations.

"LISC's capacity-mapping project literally saved my organization!" declared Shirley Simmons, executive director of Wynne Community Enlightenment and Development Corporation (EDC) in Arkansas. Wynne Community EDC was recognized in 2003 by the local LISC office at the annual conference for Delta CDCs for demonstrating the greatest capacity improvement. The executive director, board members, and the staff used the *Cap*Map process and recommendations to dramatically improve systems, processes, and practices in their organization. Simmons pointed out that the internal capacity of her organization had increased considerably and information flow had become much more dependable and accurate. Today, business decisions are being made in a more efficient and timely manner, thanks to the improvement of various systems and processes.

Reactions from LISC field offices

Across the country, LISC programs are benefiting significantly from the capacity-mapping process. Many are finding that they are able to allocate limited financial and technical resources in ways that achieve impressive results. LISC staff has reported that they are taking better advantage of the vast internal networks we have within the corporation, seeking as well as sharing innovative solutions to capacity-building challenges at an unprecedented rate. Because their ability to demonstrate concrete, verifiable results is so greatly improved, local sites are also reporting renewed interest in capacity building among their longtime funders.

Northeast Ohio LISC

In Ohio, dramatic results are evident among the twelve organizations that have participated in the local capacity-mapping program. Shelia R. Slemp, program officer for Northeast Ohio LISC, gave a report to her advisory committee in December 2003 that energized the members about *Cap*Map. After remapping her partners, Slemp found that the average financial management capacity had increased more than two stages in just over a year. Executive directors and staff of these organizations attributed much of the success to the concentrated focus on specific capacity-building activities suggested by the mapping results. That capacity increase has brought the groups organized financial information, an ability to account for all funds, and standardized internal controls for operation. Slemp points out that, "The very act of asking the CDC capacity-related questions makes them think and do things differently. They're moving forward. That's really what the biggest impact has been—changed behavior!"

Houston LISC

Amanda Timm, a program officer in Houston LISC, sees the value of *Cap*Map from a different perspective. As administrator of the organizational development program, Amanda has been mapping local groups since 2002. "We are not relying on guesswork any more. We're capturing the facts. . . . With *Cap*Map, I know and my CDCs know what matters about what they are actually doing and what more is possible. We don't just say 'LISC is your partner'; we *are* a partner. CDCs are more comfortable about asking for specific resources for specific needs, and less inclined to hide deficiencies. We can have more honest dialogues because *Cap*Map so clearly highlights next steps. Leaders are now looking beyond physical production to the organization itself. How efficient are we? How can we sustain our production? Thanks to *Cap*Map, we work together to identify gaps and correct them. From LISC's perspective, this is just what we need. We can focus on 'smart' investment—we target specific challenges."

Timm's work with more than twenty groups may be difficult at times, especially since there are so many different types of organizations in the mix—from high-performing, with a long history of accomplishment, to very young, with little or no real estate development experience. What *Cap*Map offers is a non-biased methodology that examines every organization using the exact same criteria, regardless of their age, size, or success rate.

Since *Cap*Map data reveals common needs in multiple organizations across a program site, LISC staff can now employ specialists to implement new systems and educate staff from many CDCs at the same time, instead of wasting resources by purchasing the same solutions at different times for different groups. "LISC is now seeking targeted and efficient application of resources," Timm said. "Thanks to economies of scale, we are not only saving money and energy, but also generating new opportunities that didn't exist before *Cap*Map." Timm pointed to the heavy use of peer-to-peer learning in Houston—more than ever before. Because of the information generated by *Cap*Map, she has been able to put a number of executive directors in touch with other organizations that have already instituted similar systems. This, of course, prevents one organization from spending the time and energy to develop something that may already exist in a peer group. At a minimum, more dialogue is taking place between peer organizations.

Without revealing any *Cap*Map results, LISC staff members are now in a position to do better "matchmaking." And the matchmaking opportunity is not limited to the usual CDC world. Timm regularly directs many of her CDCs to other support organizations in the region. One such organization is Texas Community Building with Attorney Resources (Texas C-BAR), which offers free legal assistance to nonprofits. When *Cap*Map reveals the need for legal advice in matters such as bylaws or policies, CDCs are referred to pro bono assistance from Texas C-BAR. Another organization, Executive Service Corps of Houston, also partners with LISC and offers free services to executive directors of many of the mapped groups. These opportunities have been more obvious and possible primarily because of the capacity-mapping program, without which it was never really possible to identify some of the trends and potential links.

> "*Cap*Map gives the local program staff a clear picture of how to move forward."
>
> — *Barbara Jeanetta, Senior Program Officer, Twin Cities LISC*

> "*Cap*Map creates the opportunity to have conversations that we just weren't having before with our partner CDCs about issues that are actually very important."
>
> — *Amanda Timm, Program Officer, Greater Houston LISC*

Next Steps and Final Words

*Cap*Map is designed to provide CDC leadership and LISC staff with a reasonable baseline measurement, a map for growth, and to help us become better, more informed consumers of relatively expensive consultant services. It is *not* a substitute for high-quality organizational assessments performed by professional providers. It is also *not* a self-assessment tool, but is an integral part of a holistic and comprehensive approach. What distinguishes this LISC brand of capacity building is a focus on results and an outcomes orientation.

*Cap*Map has the potential for industrywide scope. While enabling LISC to examine the capacity of individual CDCs, it also allows analysis on a national scale. We can aggregate the individual data into a picture of community development as a whole. We are now in the process of developing a sophisticated database tool linked to business intelligence software capable of performing advanced analysis and statistical modeling. Known as *Cap*TRACK©, this analytic system will expand LISC's research capability and enable us to

- Demonstrate the actual impact of an organization's systems capacity on the results that CDCs have produced in their communities
- Identify local, regional, and national capacity trends
- Identify which capacity-building approaches and interventions demonstrate results at different stages of organizational development
- Quantify specific growth returns for capacity-building investment dollars
- Track, model, and project CDC growth and key performance indicators over time

This represents the most ambitious research project into CDC capacity ever undertaken. We're using concrete data gathered from the hundreds of organizations we work with, examining the impact of capacity-building funding, and studying the continued growth of CDCs. While this project has clear implications for public policy debates and the allocation of private-sector resources, it will also offer technical assistance providers and funders the ability to target assistance to precise areas of organizational need.

*Cap*Map grew out of LISC's larger capacity-mapping approach, and it is integrated into LISC's business model and specific capacity-building systems. We have learned that this process requires training and support to execute effectively. As a result of this learning, and because the approach has truly helped many of the CDCs we work with, LISC is now exploring the possibility of licensing *Cap*Map (and the accompanying software now under development) in a limited fashion through pilot projects. These pilots will allow us the opportunity to explore how *Cap*Map can be executed by others, what training and ongoing support will be necessary and appropriate, and how effective it will be with a different universe of users and implementers.

By design, *Cap*Map democratizes information about organizational capacity and growth and puts it in the hands of the people who need it most: an organization's leadership and its investors. In the long term, we hope *Cap*Map will provide a rich body of data on organizational growth that will inform all of our capacity-building work. And we believe *Cap*Map may also have the potential to make a major contribution to the broader not-for-profit industry that shares many of our same capacity-building and sustainability challenges.

CHAPTER 3

The Unity Foundation's C.Q.®: Capacity Benchmarking and Capacity Building

by Dorothy E. Freeman, PhD, and Lori Roming, The Unity Foundation

The term *capacity building* still resists definitional uniformity despite more than a decade of funded interest, professional study, and hands-on practice in the philanthropic field. Capacity-oriented assessment tools of varying sophistication reflect little agreement as to what, whether, why, when, or even how to measure capacity.

The rigor and statistical reliability of tools remain generally soft despite massive investments of dollars and time by funders, consultants, and nonprofits working to build an organization's capacity. Most regrettably, the field goes wanting for a national database of capacity-building indicators cross-referenced by relevant factors such as subsector, service area, operating budget, and the like. Such indicators could be used to benchmark practices and build accountability.

We *are* making headway, as reflected by multiple approaches in this book. The existence of this book is testament to our field's persistence in the pursuit of benchmarking and building the capacity of nonprofits. To our collective credit, we are unwilling to allow capacity building simply to "come into fashion and then go out of style," to quote lyricists Calvi and Holt.[23]

---

[23] "One of Those Songs" from *Le Bal De Madame De Mortemouille*.

The Unity Foundation's Approach to Capacity Benchmarking and Capacity Building

The Unity Foundation was established in 2000 with a $5 million gift from Maine telecommunications businessman Bert G. Clifford. Unity has five fields of interest: arts/culture/recreation, community and economic development, education, environment, and youth. In 2005, the assets of this nationally focused foundation are approximately $22 million.

The Unity Foundation's mission is to invest in high-performing, sustainable nonprofits—and those with the will and readiness to become higher performing and more sustainable—through capacity-building and programmatic grants, educational institutes, technical assistance, and management support services. The Unity Foundation concentrates on three phases of capacity benchmarking and capacity building: benchmarking, intervention, and evaluation. These are linked to the Capacity Quotient (C.Q.), an online capacity-assessment tool and database designed and administered by the foundation. Figure 3, The Unity Foundation's Three-Phased Approach (page 99), illustrates the connection between benchmarking, intervention, and evaluation.

Chapter Overview

This chapter explores the development and implementation of the C.Q. (Capacity Quotient) with attention to the following topics:

- Rationale for the development of the C.Q.
- Methodology for the development of C.Q.

- C.Q. Benchmarks Report
- Use of C.Q. in grantmaking
- Unity Foundation's C.Q. Initiative
- Advice to grantmakers in funding capacity benchmarking and capacity building

---

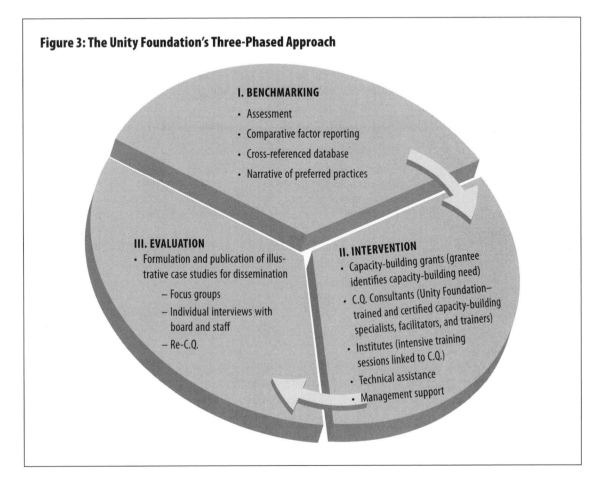

Figure 3: The Unity Foundation's Three-Phased Approach

I. BENCHMARKING
- Assessment
- Comparative factor reporting
- Cross-referenced database
- Narrative of preferred practices

III. EVALUATION
- Formulation and publication of illustrative case studies for dissemination
  - Focus groups
  - Individual interviews with board and staff
  - Re-C.Q.

II. INTERVENTION
- Capacity-building grants (grantee identifies capacity-building need)
- C.Q. Consultants (Unity Foundation–trained and certified capacity-building specialists, facilitators, and trainers)
- Institutes (intensive training sessions linked to C.Q.)
- Technical assistance
- Management support

Rationale for the Development of Capacity Quotient (C.Q.°)

When the Unity Foundation was created in 2000, we sought to be good stewards of our investments. We errantly expected to find a number of well-tested and well-accepted quantitative and qualitative capacity-assessment tools that would enable us to benchmark a nonprofit organization's capacity and determine the most appropriate investments to build capacity. When such a tool could not be found, we decided to formally research, test, and develop our own capacity benchmarking and building instrument (along with a cross-referenced database) to guide our work as a foundation.

Our goal was to formulate a reliable assessment for capacity benchmarking and to build a database to contribute to existing efforts to foster higher performing nonprofits. Simply stated, the goal of Unity Foundation's capacity benchmarking and building program is to enable nonprofits to strengthen their management capacity and, as a result, their mission capacity.

How we developed the tool

Two central goals guide the mission of the foundation in its relationship with nonprofit partners: investing in nonprofits to build ever-higher performance of their laser-like missions, and achieving sustainability so that nonprofits can fulfill their missions over the long haul. These same goals guided our development methodology.

First, we began a twenty-seven-month process of identifying the capacity characteristics of high-performing, sustainable nonprofits. Second, we invited the counsel of field experts in nonprofit accounting, fundraising, technology, governance, marketing, operations, communications, and law. Third, we researched the most compelling scholarship on capacity building. Fourth, based on that blend of expertise in practice and theory, an assessment tool was designed as an online, password-protected, and statistically grounded tool. This tool was tested, refined, and retested. From that assessment tool—C.Q.—a database was derived that captured the responses of board and executive staff members along with supporting quantitative data such as annual operating budgets and the number of staff and board members.

Features of the tool

Two features distinguish our instrument's approach to benchmarking capacity: it is board-driven rather than staff-driven, and it is readiness-based rather than life-cycle-based. *Board-driven* refers to the legal and practical duty of the board to ensure the capacity necessary to fulfill the nonprofit's mission. *Readiness* refers to the willingness of board and executive staff to engage fully and actively in the commitment of resources required to systematically build a nonprofit's management capacity.

The C.Q. tool—which takes approximately thirty-five minutes to complete—measures four primary indicators linked to performance and sustainability: leadership, advancement, treasury, and operations. During the twenty-seven-month process of examining capacity, these four indicators emerged as the four legs that supported a nonprofit organization. Each indicator depends on the other and cannot stand alone. An advantage of limiting the indicators to four is that the instrument is less demanding of those who complete it. Most people are not prepared to spend hours taking a survey. Each of these indicators contains three subindicators, listed and defined below.

Capacity: a continuous process of attracting and managing finite board-ensured resources on a rapidly changing landscape to produce projects, programs, services, and activities that are demonstrably appropriate to the nonprofit's mission.

Because the lexicon of capacity has been constructed with rather loose definitions, C.Q. states definitions with each term for clarity. The following list of definitions begins with our operational definition of capacity and includes the definitions for the indicators and subindicators that the tool measures.

Capacity: a three-part, continuous process of

- *Attracting and managing finite board-ensured resources* (both human and capital)
- on a *rapidly changing landscape*
- to produce projects, programs, services, and activities that are *demonstrably appropriate to the nonprofit's mission.*

I. *Leadership:* A fully informed board vesting itself and the executive staff with the authority and responsibility to execute the organization's precise mission with discipline.

A. *Mission:* what the nonprofit concretely does for whom—not abstractions—for example, raison d'etre, values, or spirit

B. *Board:* directors or trustees of a nonprofit organization with the fiduciary responsibility and legal liability to act in the best interest of the organization

C. *Executive staff:* under the direction of the chief executive officer, the executive staff—CEO, CFO, CDO—having board-delegated authority and responsibility to manage the organization

II. *Advancement:* A board-engaged system for gaining assent for the nonprofit organization's mission using strategic communication assets designed to inform and persuade key constituencies (donors, clients, media, policymakers, funders, and the general public).

A. *Fundraising:* securing individual and institutional financial resources to fulfill the nonprofit's stated mission of what it does for whom

B. *Marketing:* time, talent, and treasury voluntarily provided by key publics—donors, clients, media, policymakers, funders, and the general public—in exchange for tangible and intangible benefits provided by the nonprofit

C. *Communications:* systematic, consistent storytelling by a nonprofit to its key publics of what it does for whom

III. *Treasury:* Partnership of board and executive director to ensure the fiduciary obligations associated with fiscal policymaking, budget formation, resource generation, financial management, and compliance.

A. *Planning and budgeting:* the nonprofit's plan to fulfill its mission expressed in terms of dollars

B. *Financial management:* financial analysis and forecasting in combination with cash, investment, borrowing, and banking management

C. *Financial reporting:* numeric and narrative management tools that testify to a nonprofit's internal financial position, results of activities, cash flows, and external accountability

IV. *Operations:* The equation whereby the right people plus the right tools plus the right programs equal high mission performance and sustainability.

A. *Human resource management:* paid staff and unpaid volunteers—including board members—who put a nonprofit's mission into practice

B. *Infrastructure:* board-ensured facilities and technology required to fulfill a nonprofit's mission

C. *Program management:* programs, projects, services, and activities used in direct fulfillment of a nonprofit's mission

C.Q. consists of sixty questions, with each having four potential responses— "definitely so," "probably so," "probably not so," and "not so." C.Q. includes fifteen questions of organizational readiness to tackle capacity building—to our mind the foremost predictor of success in capacity building. E-mail correspondence with Paul Shoemaker, director of Social Venture Partners Seattle, reaffirmed our experience: "Internal readiness to tackle [capacity building] is success factor number one. We reinforce that heartily," he wrote.

A description of C.Q. appears on the Unity Foundation web site at http://www. unityfdn.org. To avoid skewing the responses, the actual questions cannot be viewed until board and executive staff members are actually taking C.Q. For research purposes, however, the Unity Foundation can be contacted directly with inquiries.

A word about readiness: for comparative analysis, several of the readiness-based questions on C.Q. were selected for cross-tabulation with Paul Light's work, *Sustaining Nonprofit Performance*.[24] It is noteworthy that the responses of board members and executive staff members who completed C.Q. widely diverged from the responses of "opinion leaders" and "executive directors" in the Light study on questions concerning the relationship between a nonprofit "being well managed" and "effective in achieving program goals." Such divergence is a rich source for further study that may bear significant heuristic value for future practice and research in our collective understanding of capacity building. From our research, many (if not most) nonprofits recognize the need to build their management capacity to enhance their performance and sustainability. Yet only a fraction report the requisite readiness of board and staff to engage in the intensive, incremental, and long-term activities associated with capacity-building.

Reports from the tool

A nonprofit pays $495 to take C.Q. and receive the C.Q. Benchmarks Report. Special rates have been developed for unique situations. The fee covers only a portion of the foundation's costs of C.Q., but it represents the essential co-investment by a nonprofit in benchmarking an organization's capacity.

---

[24] Paul Charles Light, *Sustaining Nonprofit Performance : The Case for Capacity Building and the Evidence to Support It* (Washington, DC: Brookings Institution Press, 2004)

Several nonprofits have reported substantial success in securing capacity funding from various sources by leveraging their C.Q. assessment. Nonprofits have also used C.Q. to target areas needing strengthening that inform their board recruitment efforts. And several grantmakers have adopted C.Q. as part of their funding process as a strategic means of benchmarking and building capacity among their grantees.

A nonprofit must require total participation by the board and executive staff in order to receive its C.Q. Benchmarks Report.

After the nonprofit completes the online instrument, a fifty-page C.Q. Benchmarks Report is transmitted electronically to the board chair and the executive director. The report

- Scores responses on all factors numerically and iconically

- Compares scores on each item with all other nonprofits that have taken C.Q.

- Proffers a statement of "preferred practice" on all factors

- Calculates a group score on each primary and subindicator as well as an overall capacity score

- Contains an executive summary of the scores of all factors in the report

C.Q.® Benchmarks Report Analysis

In addition to the C.Q. benchmarks indicating how the board and executive staff scored their own organization on performance-linked capacity indicators, an accompanying C.Q. benchmark shows the aggregated average C.Q. benchmark for all nonprofits that completed C.Q. to date.

For each capacity indicator, there is a *preferred practice* of nonprofit management (drawn from contributions to the field from management practice, applied research, organizational theory, and nonprofit scholarship). If responses from the nonprofit's board and executive staff scored a statistical average of greater than or equal to 3.00, it is benchmarked as three rings out from preferred practice on a given factor. If the score is 2.00–2.99, it is benchmarked as two rings out from preferred practice on that factor. If the score is 1.10–1.99, it is benchmarked as one ring out from preferred practice on the specific factor. Scores of 1.00–1.09 are benchmarked in the "bulls-eye" of preferred practice. The bulls-eye is challenging to achieve and indicates a fully engaged board (and executive staff) that ensures the human and capital resources needed to fulfill a laser-focused mission of the nonprofit organization.

In addition to the fifty-page C.Q. Benchmarks Report, an organization will receive a five-page C.Q. Benchmarks Report Analysis. This analysis addresses each primary indicator and shows the quick version of responses and the ring level achieved. Figure 4, Sample Abbreviated Benchmarks Report, shows an abbreviated format of the analysis for a fictional nonprofit.

Figure 4. Sample Abbreviated Benchmarks Report

C.Q.® Capacity Quotient Benchmarks Report: Nonprofit X

INDICATORS	Nonprofit X	Average of all Orgs	Distance from Bulls-eye	1 Ring Out	2 Ring Outs	3 Ring Outs
OVERALL	2.35	1.96	1.26		X	
I. Leadership	1.79	1.54	0.70	X		
A. Mission	1.81	1.65	0.72	X		
B. Board	1.94	1.50	0.85	X		
C. Executive Staff	1.60	1.46	0.51	X		
II. Advancement	2.63	1.95	1.54		X	
A. Fundraising	3.04	2.05	1.95			X
B. Marketing	2.53	1.99	1.44		X	
C. Communications	2.31	1.82	1.22		X	
III. Treasury	2.60	2.31	1.51		X	
A. Planning and Budgeting	2.86	2.54	1.77		X	
B. Financial Management	2.50	2.17	1.41		X	
C. Financial Reporting	2.44	2.21	1.35		X	
IV. Operations	2.39	2.06	1.30		X	
A. Human Resource Management	1.99	1.90	0.90	X		
B. Infrastructure	2.97	2.38	1.88		X	
C. Program Management	2.21	1.89	1.12		X	

After reviewing the C.Q. Benchmarks Report, a nonprofit's board determines which aspect of capacity-building to address—although we encourage taking one key aspect at a time. As a grantmaker, our interest is in the proposed plan to address the problem area they judge to be their priority.

Upon completion of C.Q., a nonprofit should address these four questions in order to develop a funding application:

1. What did C.Q. reveal as the foremost capacity-building need that your organization is ready to address?

2. What is your plan?

3. What budget is required for your plan?

4. How will you know that you have made "progress-against-plan" on this capacity factor?

Using C.Q.® to Support Grantmaking

In August 2002, the Unity Foundation announced a capacity-building initiative titled C.Q. Initiative. Approximately 200 board and executive staff members from 162 nonprofits in Maine, Massachusetts, New Hampshire, Vermont, Maryland, and California attended the required orientation to learn about C.Q. and the initiative's purposes. The goal of the C.Q. Initiative was to learn lessons about how to better use the assessment tool as part of the grantmaking process. Three goals of the C.Q. Initiative included

1. Using C.Q. to benchmark existing capacity in nonprofit organizations

2. Investing in capacity-building plans of a group of nonprofits at five funding levels ($5,000; $7,500; $10,000; $15,000; and $20,000) for a period of twelve months

3. Assessing capacity building "progress-against-plan" after twelve months (using multiple peer learning experiences and an illustrative case study for each organization)

Seventy-seven nonprofits in Maine, Massachusetts, New Hampshire, and Vermont completed C.Q. for a C.Q. Benchmarks Report to be issued. Of that group, sixty-three nonprofits submitted a capacity-building plan and grant request of up to $20,000 over a twelve-month period to build capacity in a key area identified by their C.Q. Benchmarks Report.

From the sixty-three plans submitted, fifteen nonprofits received capacity-building grants. The forty-eight nonprofits that had applied but were not chosen for the C.Q. Initiative received an offer of an unrestricted grant of $250. These small grants were offered as a means of providing unrestricted funding and to determine whether nonprofits that had completed C.Q. would avail themselves of a grant that would help them recover more than half of the C.Q. fee of $495. Surprisingly, only seventeen nonprofits (35 percent) took advantage of the opportunity.

C.Q.® Initiative objectives

The C.Q. Initiative was designed to evaluate the C.Q. instrument in benchmarking key capacity indicators with a small number of nonprofits over a twelve-month period. Nonprofits were selected on the basis of their plans to focus on a concrete aspect of capacity building. Proposals were limited by time frame (one year) and budget (not to exceed $20,000). During that twelve-month period, nonprofits also committed to work with Unity Foundation by attending three peer-learning events and reporting their experiences for inclusion in a compendium of C.Q. illustrative case studies.

Objectives of the C.Q. Initiative included

1. Creating a database of key capacity indicators (with breakdowns according to subsector, geographic service area, operating budget, board size, and number of employees)

2. Assessing capacity-building outcomes within various levels of funding

3. Producing capacity-building case studies to disseminate lessons learned

4. Refining the Unity Foundation's grantmaking effectiveness in capacity building through accurate diagnosis (C.Q.) and intervention (funding, technical assistance, and management support services)

Fifteen nonprofit organizations with annual operating budgets from $57,000 to $10,500,000 were selected for the C.Q. Initiative.

In the second year of the C.Q. Initiative (in which thirteen of the original fifteen nonprofits participated), the cohort was challenged to engage in jointly funding their capacity-building plan's second phase. For grant requests less than $5,000, nonprofits were to match 50 percent of the amount given by the foundation. For grant requests greater than $5,000, nonprofits were to contribute an amount at least equal to that given by the foundation.

Lessons grantees learned from the initiative

The following examples are grant reports from grantees that highlight important capacity lessons learned. Each organization was represented by a "peer" (that is, executive director, director of development, etc.) and a board chair or president. Here is a synopsis of the lessons learned by nonprofits from the initiative.[25]

Ashwood Waldorf School (Rockport, ME)

Ashwood Waldorf School provides prenursery through eighth grade education and exposes children to classic academic teachings, the arts, and community service. The Unity Foundation awarded the school $5,000 to conduct a marketing audit to identify current marketing opportunities and to develop a three-phased prioritized action plan.

Lessons learned

The most urgent capacity-building challenge confronting the school was in the area of development. With a capacity-building grant, the school was able to develop a successful development effort. Key milestones included

- Hiring a development director
- Successfully launching a challenge campaign that raised more than $40,000 to support the construction of new office space, purchase computer equipment and software, and fund a capital campaign feasibility study
- Developing a fundraising plan that called for increases in annual giving, an expansion of the donor pool, and increased foundation funding

---

[25] The reports that follow are in the respondent's own words. Grantees have given permission to publish their remarks.

This work resulted in a 115 percent increase in annual giving for two consecutive years; a jump in school community participation in annual giving from 45 percent to 97 percent; an increase in the number of nonschool community donors; and a sharp increase in foundation funding.

From a peer perspective, the process has demonstrated the value of carefully identifying and prioritizing capacity challenges and developing well-defined, achievable plans of action to address those challenges. The addition of new staff without sufficient anticipation of space and equipment needs seems to be a repetitive error and one that needs to be avoided in the future.

Sunrise County Economic Council (Machias, ME)

Sunrise County Economic Council (SCEC) is a countywide cooperative that promotes the community and economic development of Downeast Maine. The Unity Foundation awarded them $20,000 to support a development professional to raise program funds and manage SCEC's endowment campaign.

Lessons learned

Through its capacity-building efforts, Unity Foundation has brought us a long way toward becoming and remaining a viable economic stimulus for our service area. Participation [in the CQ Initiative] has revealed our strong and weak points. It has allowed us to glean knowledge from similar groups and/or other new organizations experiencing similar problems.

Through the C.Q. efforts, our board has learned more about itself, its makeup, and the goals we want to accomplish. Self-evaluation stimulated by the Unity Foundation has helped greatly in this effort. Through this effort we have modified our approach at board meetings. We have separated into committees with assignments, which allows more thorough evaluations of what we are doing.

Participation in C.Q. and using the C.Q. grant we received has provided the financial capability for our staff and director to have the time to help us plan as an organization rather than having to allocate time based on the immediate needs of a specific program.

The greatest learning experience for me has been the conscious effort the staff and board have made to recruit new board members who will strengthen our team and make a contribution. The result of this effort has already been noticed in recent board meetings as the new board members have made a tremendous contribution. The board as a whole is more informed, engaged, and effective.

Thomas College (Waterville, ME)

Thomas College is a business-focused institution of higher learning in central Maine. The Unity Foundation awarded the college $15,000 to research, formulate, and implement a formal brand charter.

It was important to examine the college's mission and develop a comprehensive and coordinated marketing and communications strategy. This strategy would capture the college's brand and initiate other strategies for promulgating it.

Greatest learning experience—board chair's response

It is my perception that 100 percent participation from the board of trustees in the C.Q. Initiative had a critical impact on our outcomes, as did my mandatory attendance at conferences and workshops. The branding committee involved board members in choosing a final consultant and throughout the branding initiative with [the marketing consultant we chose]. Unfortunately, the client executive assigned to us resigned from [the marketing consultant] before completing the project.

I developed a new appreciation for the value of quality board members. Success depends upon the constant enhancement of all core college constituents. We learned that the quality of the governing board especially will have the greatest long-term impact on the college. Thus, we have formed, for the first time, a board resources (or nominating) committee.

Advice to Grantmakers Interested in Funding Capacity Benchmarking and Capacity Building

Funders interested in grantmaking to benchmark and build the management capacity of nonprofits are greatly needed in the philanthropy field. Based upon the experience of the Unity Foundation and the responses of participants in the initiative, the following advice is offered:

- Remember that ensuring capacity is the legal duty of the board

- Begin with an accurate assessment of existing capacity

- Look carefully at the board's readiness for capacity building

- Provide incremental funding for multiple years

- Support and convene peer-learning opportunities among capacity-building grantees

- Disseminate lessons learned so other nonprofits and funders understand how and why capacity benchmarking and capacity building is essential

Building capacity is a continuous process. It cannot simply be "done" and put to one side. Capacity must be reviewed systematically so that board members, staff members, volunteers, and potential funders understand your mission, how you plan to carry out your mission, and how you can record the effectiveness of your programs.

If you would like additional information about C.Q., please contact Unity Foundation at http://www.unityfdn.org.

CHAPTER 4

Assessing the Capacity of Grassroots Organizations

based on interviews with Gladys Washington and Kathie deNobriga of
Mary Reynolds Babcock Foundation

Imagine you are the newly appointed executive director of a grassroots Latino advocacy organization in the southeastern United States. The organization is community based: its ideas, energy, and support come from the local Latino community, and stakeholders are involved with planning and decision making. The majority of your board members are adjusting to life in a new country as well as learning the ropes of board service. As executive director, you want to lead the organization in building capacity and securing adequate funding, but the organization faces several unique barriers that make this difficult to achieve. How should the organization negotiate the opinions of its many stakeholders and numerous other language, cultural, and technical challenges it faces?

From its work with grassroots organizations dealing with issues of class and race in the Southeast, the Mary Reynolds Babcock Foundation of Winston-Salem, NC, has learned that organizational development for these small new organizations would require a unique approach.

The mission of the Mary Reynolds Babcock Foundation is to assist people in the Southeast to build just and caring communities that nurture individuals, spur enterprise, bridge differences, foster fairness, and promote civility. Recognizing the debilitating impact of persistent poverty and racism on community life in the region, the foundation seeks progress in areas where poverty prevails and race divides. The foundation's resources are concentrated in four primary grantmaking areas: grassroots leadership development, community problem solving, enterprise and asset development, and organizational development.

The Organizational Development program began in 1995 to strengthen the effectiveness and sustainability of organizations across the Southeast whose missions match the foundation's purpose and values. The foundation encouraged applicants in each grantmaking program to include specific organizational development goals, work plans, and budgets in their proposals. To increase organizations' capacity to achieve their goals, the foundation conducted annual gatherings that offered peer training and networking around organizational development issues.

When the foundation first started working with community grassroots organizations in 2001, we quickly discovered that these organizations required a different level of technical assistance than older and larger organizations. Many community organizations are located in rural areas with no access to technical support. Typically, these organizations have not worked with large foundations before. In addition, they often need help in identifying what areas of their operations require outside support and assistance. We've learned that building capacity in these organizations requires an open and honest relationship, an understanding of the organization's life stage, and flexibility throughout the grant process. We hope our style of working with grantees has been beneficial to them because it is different from the typical grantor-grantee relationship.

Chapter Overview

The Babcock Foundation's organizational assessment is integrated with a learning and evaluation plan that is part of every grant to grassroots organizations. This chapter will

- Provide an overview of the Babcock Foundation's grantmaking and assessment process for grassroots organizations
- Share lessons learned
- Describe the benefits of partnering with third-party intermediaries when conducting an organizational assessment

- Explain the foundation's values and philosophy on building strong relationships with grantees
- Share two success stories from the foundation's grassroots organization portfolio

The CD-ROM that accompanies this book includes the following materials to support this chapter:

- *Framework for the Mary Reynolds Babcock Foundation's GRO Grantees*
- *GRO Program Learning and Evaluation Forms*

Grantmaking and Assessment Process for Grassroots Organizations

The Mary Reynolds Babcock Foundation funds a pool of twelve to sixteen grassroots organizations annually. Grantees receive eighteen-month renewable grants for up to three years. The average grant size ranges from $30,000 to $45,000 over eighteen months, which is significant for small organizations having budgets under $300,000.

Before an organization has submitted an official proposal, program officers work with applicants to develop an initial learning and evaluation plan for both programs and organizational development and where grantees have to describe their eighteen-month and three-year goals. Each organization must answer three questions:

1. What is the change you're looking for?

2. How will you get there?

3. How will you know it's been achieved?

This exercise helps grantees look toward the change rather than the outcome or the activities. For example, a grantee might say it wants to have twelve board members rather than eight—but chances are what they really want is stronger governance or access to more funds. The program officer helps the grantee identify the underlying change behind activities like increasing board size.

The program officer pushes for clarity on the results the grantee expects to achieve toward each goal as well as activities they plan to undertake to achieve those results. Finally, the grantee must consider what evidence it will collect to know whether it has achieved desired results. By pushing for clarity on the evidence and results the grantee seeks, the program officer is helping the grantee test the logic of its thinking. Figure 5, Example Learning and Evaluation Plan (page 116), shows how one organization answered the three questions.

The learning and evaluation form puts ownership and control of outcomes squarely in the grantee's lap. Foundation staff and consultants may offer advice for completing the learning and evaluation form, but the organization's board

---

Figure 5. Example Learning and Evaluation Plan

Activities: Two board trainings of fundraising; implementation of a series of house parties for members

Evidence: 90 percent of the board attends training (pre- and post-training survey indicated increased comfort with fundraising); 75 percent of board members host a house party or invite members to participate; able to raise $10,000 from individuals

3-Year Goal: To raise 20 percent of our budget from members

18-Month Result: The board is more comfortable and active in annual fundraising campaign, raising $10,000 from members

---

and staff are encouraged to work together to complete the form so there is ownership of the anticipated results and activities. The grantee is not being held to someone else's standards. Once completed, the form reflects the mutual agreement on the results for which the foundation will hold the grantee accountable. We understand that flexibility is key, so grantees are allowed to change their learning and evaluation plans as they learn more through the assessment and implementation process.

Once an organization has been approved for funding, the foundation engages a consultant to serve as a resource broker—an intermediary between the foundation and the grantee. The resource broker usually then hires an independent consultant to partner with the grantee in conducting an organizational capacity assessment. The purpose of the assessment process is to gain understanding of the strengths and weaknesses of the organization. The intent is to help each organization do one of three things:

1. To affirm that their own internal instincts and assessments are on target

2. To offer a different take on what their organizational needs are, in which case we would recommend they redo their learning and evaluation plan

3. To see how their needs are interconnected and think about where strategic action could possibly address multiple areas

The assessment process is *not* used as a tool to pull funding or to dictate how organizational development funds should be spent.

Development of the assessment tool

The Babcock Foundation's assessment tool was inspired by and adapted from tools created at the Center for Community Change and the Center for Nonprofits in Georgia. It is being developed as a diagnostic and learning tool to assess an organization along the twelve "core components" of organizational development as the foundation and its grantees have described: mission, vision, values; resource development; strategic planning; program development; learning and evaluation; human resources; legal/fiscal compliance; management systems; governance; organizational culture; collaborations, and constituent relationships. The assessment tool, a work-in-progress, organizes these components into seven broad capacity areas and provides key indicators:

1. Planning

2. Fundraising

3. Board development and governance

4. Human resources

5. Financial management

6. Evaluation

7. Communications and technology

In each area, the tool lists indicators of strong capacity. Recognizing the unique challenges start-up and growing organizations face, the tool also provides questions assessors can ask of start-up or growing organizations to help gauge whether their capacity is adequate for the organization's life stage. Also key to the assessment and to the foundation's understanding about organizational development is a keen attention to and respect for the context in which the organization is working.

The assessments are based on a review of materials, interviews, and group discussion. The assessor, an outside consultant, will have confidential conversations with key board and staff members to discuss the strengths, weaknesses, and challenges of the organization. Following the interviews, the assessor prepares a draft of the report, which includes a summary of the conversations, and meets with the organization to discuss the summary and identify the key areas to address. At this point, the grantee and consultant can work together to make changes to the report. Going over the draft with the consultant is often a significant learning moment for the grantee.

Within a month after the organization has discussed the findings with the consultant, the organization discusses the assessment with the resource broker. This gives some time for the organization to gain additional insight into the evaluation results and also gives the resource broker an opportunity to read and reflect on the assessment and review the original proposal. The completed report will then be given to the organization to incorporate with its learning and evaluation plan and to the foundation. At this time, the grantee can make changes to its learning and evaluation plan, based on the findings of the assessment. We work to structure the process so that it is appropriate and meaningful to the grantees. We do not want our grantees to feel like they are going through the motions of something just because it was in the original grant proposal. We also try to emphasize continual learning and focus on organizational development. We usually call our grantees six months into the grant cycle to remind them that now would be a good time to look over their budget and goals and determine whether they need to make a change to their learning and evaluation plan.

Lessons Learned

Our work in the Organizational Development program has taught us many valuable lessons. These lessons help shape our values and our interactions with our grantees. The lessons come into play during the assessment and throughout the grant process.

1. *Organizational development grants are one way to fulfill the foundation's purpose and values.* By investing in organizations whose missions and impact are consistent with the foundation's priorities, we can further our own mission to help build just and caring communities.

2. *Organizational development is a wise strategic investment.* Experience has shown that organizational development work is significant in improving grantees' effectiveness. Previous grantees have told us they may not have

survived if they had not addressed internal management, human development, program development, and funding issues through their organizational development work.

3. *The impact of organizational development work is difficult to evaluate.* To judge the impact of organizational development grants, the foundation has relied upon external evaluation with targeted questions, grantee self-reports, firsthand conversations between staff and grantees, and observations.

4. *Nonprofits need financial support to become effective organizations.* By excluding operating costs and organizational development work from project grants, foundations jeopardize the impact of projects and limit organizations' long-term effectiveness.

5. *Nonprofits are skeptical and unaccustomed to foundations investing in more than their projects.* Over the years, the Babcock Foundation has had to teach, prod, and monitor nonprofits as they tread new organizational development ground. More important, we have had to work diligently at building relationships of trust with grantees to convince them that we are committed to building their effectiveness and sustainability for the long term.

6. *The time and circumstances have to be right for an organization to tackle significant organizational development work.* Small-scale organizational development projects can spur modest improvement, but the kind of organizational development work that builds organizational competency and furthers program effectiveness requires the buy-in and commitment of board and staff.

7. *There is power in convening grantees for peer learning and support.* The organizational development program included an annual gathering of grantees to share lessons from their struggles to improve their impact and strengthen their organizations. Because this was such a successful gathering we have continued similar types of convenings with our grassroots grantees. Such opportunities offer moral support and create formal and informal alliances among peers to support program and organizational development work. Anecdotal evidence tells us that some of these peer relationships have outlasted formal participation in our program.

8. *The foundation and grantees have learned to be flexible with and accountable to each other.* At the beginning of each grant, we negotiate specific organizational development outcomes and determine what evidence will be collected to assess progress. Since organizational development work does not always proceed as planned, we renegotiate activities and budgets as necessary, according to what the organization is learning and achieving. Feedback from grantees gained during these exchanges and through the external evaluation has improved and shaped the direction of the organizational development program.

9. *Deeper relationships between the foundation and grantees have resulted from our longer-term investment, shared learning, and mutual accountability.* The foundation and grantees know and trust each other enough to serve as mutual resources for advice.

10. *The foundation has been more supportive of grantees' organizational development work because we are committed to our own ongoing organizational development work.* By being deeply engaged in our own clarification of purpose and values, strategic planning, board development, staff restructuring, policy development, and evaluation, we have learned along with grantees as organizational development practitioners.

Relying on Third-Party Intermediaries

The assessment process and the work that comes after rely on the use of outside consultants. The resource broker is the main point of contact in working with the grantees to help guide and assess progress. The resource broker assigns an assessor and recommends appropriate consultants. These consultants help create the appropriate distance between the Babcock Foundation and grantees. Assessors and consultants can identify challenges and articulate frustrations the staff has been trying to say for years but may have been unable to pinpoint. Although the assessors help the grantees identify their areas of need, the grantees are the ones who ultimately negotiate and choose which consultants they will partner with for their technical assistance needs. For instance, the resource broker or the assessor may identify vendors that are likely to be a good fit for each grantee, but the grantees are the ones who choose whom they will work with and negotiate the precise terms of engagement.

We work with a large pool of consultants and try to find a good match for each organization. We try to make sure the consultants understand the type of organization they are working with so they will show care and respect for the organization. In addition, the foundation created an application process for the consultants conducting the assessment to ensure consultants understand the dynamics of working with grassroots organizations in the South and the unique challenges of race, class, and culture that consultants must be sensitive to. Through this process and the straightforward style of the tool itself, the foundation is able to mitigate the risk of having consultants do harm within organizations. One way we screen our consultants is to ask, What are the first three questions you would ask a board member about a certain topic (like planning)? It can be illuminating to see how people would approach the work differently.

In addition to helping with the assessment and learning and evaluation plans, consultants can provide tremendous benefit to organizations who may have never had access to this type of expertise before. Many board members of these organizations have never served on a board or held other leadership positions in the community. They may be overcoming oppressive practices from generations back. Educating them about board service at the same time is a daunting challenge. By modeling behaviors, consultants can help these board members come out of their shells. The assessors can model asking good questions, respectful listening and getting feedback from everyone.

Building Relationships with Grantees

Relationship building is a large part of our work. In order for the Babcock Foundation to be the best grantmaker it can be, we need to understand the issues our grantees are facing. If grantees try to block information from the foundation, they limit Babcock's effectiveness. Fortunately, this has not been a problem: out of the more than fifty organizations that have completed an assessment, only one has had concerns about sharing the information with the foundation.

A pivotal element to the success of the assessment tool is the level of confidentiality between the consultant and the grantees. This confidentiality allows a nonintimidating forum for grantees to voice any dissatisfaction they may experience in working with the foundation.

Grantees generally have been quite receptive to the assessment. First, they are usually ecstatic to be getting such a significant amount of money so they are more amenable to our process. In addition, the proper framing has helped make the grantee perception positive. The tool has been presented with the message that it is part of their support. There are no surprises when the assessment begins; they know it is part of the grant conditions, and we work to be flexible with them so they can keep ownership of the results and their learning and evaluation plans.

The foundation's experience thus far has shown that grantees are primarily honest in their communications. Further, the design of the Learning and Evaluation tool—and the fact that it is tied strongly to measurable outcomes—helps identify any potential discrepancies or contradictions in grantee reporting.

Stories of Success

Latino Advocacy Coalition of Henderson County, NC

The Latino Advocacy Coalition (LAC) was formed in 1998 by a group of community members, educators, service providers, and clergy. Today LAC is a 501(c)(3) organization with two staff members. In addition to providing some services and leadership development, LAC publishes *El Contacto,* a monthly Spanish newsletter, and holds El Consejo, a monthly meeting open to the community, which provides leadership, oversight, and guidance for LAC. LAC's first major endeavor was the creation of a Latino Community Center, El Centro, which opened in July 2002. El Centro provides shared space for LAC and four other organizations that serve the Latino community. At the time of the assessment the executive director had been on staff for eleven months, and the organization was working to build organizational capacity, systems, and adequate funding.

Strengths

LAC is a community-based organization whose ideas, energy, and support come from the Latino community in Henderson County. The board of directors' membership is 70 percent Latino, and the Consejo meeting structure ensures that a broad base of community members are involved with planning and decision making. In interviews conducted during the assessment, several stakeholders said LAC is the point of connection for individuals and programs wishing to connect with the Latino community. During the assessor's visit, the center was lively and filled with Latino people of all ages—families with young children seemed to have come for a meeting, teenagers were working in the computer lab, and adults ages twenty to sixty were there to meet with the immigration lawyers. It was clear that the community center is actively used and a place that people come to gather, attend workshops, receive services, and participate in programming. Furthermore, the staff and board members who participated in the assessment interviews were energetic, enthusiastic, and filled with ideas about how to develop LAC, expand programming, and better serve the community.

Key challenges

As both staff and board members were quick to identify, LAC's community-based nature is both its greatest strength and greatest challenge. The organization has a great deal of energy and many ideas for expansion. During interviews, individuals mentioned their hopes for a more developed youth program, a permanent building for LAC, expanded advocacy programs, various plans for fundraising events, and leadership development and training for board and staff. There did not seem to be a single, cohesive, shared vision for how LAC would develop or which issues should be tackled in what order. As several individuals explained, the grassroots nature of LAC and its board has led to challenges in fundraising, sharing information, and developing depth of board leadership.

Recommended plan for organizational development

The assessor's recommendations for organizational development fell into five broad categories:

1. Strengthen governance by providing board training, developing a committee structure, and designing a recruitment strategy to expand and diversify board membership

2. Conduct a strategic planning process to ensure LAC leadership has a shared vision and goals

3. Improve financial systems and reporting to satisfy funders and clearly present financial information to board and staff

4. Develop a fundraising plan to determine how the organization will meet the goals laid out in the strategic plan

5. Develop a system for effectively managing volunteers so that the energy of stakeholders can be put to the best use

Implementation

Based on the recommendations in the assessment, the Latino Advocacy Coalition made the following changes:

- The organization disbanded an advisory group and blended it into the board structure to increase the board size and give the board greater Latino representation

- The organization conducted two board retreats that resulted in a board-led grassroots fundraising plan

- The board created a committee to develop systems for constituent input and involvement

- Staff and board created personnel policies and procedures

- The executive director received training in grant writing and financial management

Outcomes

The LAC's organizational development work led to several improvements. After the changes in board structure, the board was made up primarily of Latino members, which is more representative of the organization's constituency. Also, the board began to assume responsibility for fundraising, which improved the organization's fundraising performance. Finally, the organization had better financial management in place, thanks to the training the executive director received.

Concerned Citizens for a Better Tunica County (CCBTC), Tunica, MS

Tunica County is a poor rural county with fewer than 10,000 people. Although the population is 70 percent African American, the local power structure is still controlled by whites. Community leaders began organizing under the CCBTC name around 1993 to empower local residents to take a more active role in local decision making. In 1996, CCBTC played a major role in preventing the diversion of public funds to build what would have been an all-white school in the community. This victory energized the group to become formally incorporated. In 1999 the organization established a youth leadership component—Tunica Teens in Action—which now boasts membership of more than one hundred young people. Today, CCBTC plays a key watchdog role in the community.

Strengths

The organizational assessment found that CCBTC has strong and committed staff leadership and exceptional youth leaders. The executive director has ensured that decision making is open and participatory and that information is fully shared. It is clear that if he were not around, the organization would be able to continue and grow because of the leadership that has been cultivated. The perception among the youth interviewed is that without CCBTC, the voice of African-American residents would be almost nonexistent in local decision making. The strong youth component promises a bright future for CCBTC; the leadership being nurtured now will ensure there will be a cadre of strong and committed members and organizational leaders.

Concerns

The assessor noted concern that few CCBTC adult members openly identify themselves as such. While it is understandable that, given the local history of violence and oppression against African Americans who "spoke out," people may be afraid to be publicly associated with a group like CCBTC, the organization seems to be challenged by this anonymous participation. In addition to this cultural challenge, the assessor also noted some infrastructure challenges, such as a weak accounting system, lack of a personnel policies manual, too much dependence on foundation grants, and conflicts of interest on the board.

Recommended plan for organizational development

The assessor found that CCBTC was at a point of its development where more formal systems needed to be developed to facilitate organizational growth. The assessment included the following recommendations in four areas for organizational development:

1. *Management and administration.* Develop a computerized accounting system and train staff how to use it. Develop a personnel manual.

2. *Fundraising.* Develop a fundraising plan that includes a goal to diversify funding. Provide fundraising training for board and staff members. Hire a consultant to explore the development of a workplace-giving program with local casinos.

3. *Board development.* Train board members on roles and responsibilities. Create a board development plan. Engage the board in strategic planning for the organization.

4. *Organizing.* Develop an outreach plan to increase membership.

Implementation

CCBTC implemented the assessment's recommendations in the following ways:

• *Management and administration.* Staff received systems management training and new financial management software to provide better reports for the board. Some board members received computer training so they could do the hands-on work of the organization if needed.

- *Board development.* CCBTC decided to restructure the board to remove staff from it. The organization had an intergenerational governance structure including youth board members to represent its large youth constituency. However, after receiving rules and responsibilities training, the board decided its youth board members should be at least eighteen years of age so that they could have the same level of responsibility as adult board members. The board also received training in reviewing financial reports so that it could be more accountable in providing financial oversight.

Outcomes

The staff training and changes made to governance structure improved the organization's financial management systems and made the board more accountable with a clearer separation of duties between board and staff.

Conclusion

While conducting a capacity assessment is a helpful way for us to prioritize our organizational development work with grantees, it is just one part of a highly engaged relationship. If our capacity assessment tool were used on its own without appropriate setup or follow-up, it could possibly cause more harm than good.

The Babcock Foundation prides itself on open communications with grantees and flexibility throughout the grants process. Conducting an organizational assessment using a third-party intermediary is extremely helpful in getting an honest take on grantees' capacity challenges and finding the most appropriate ways to partner with them on organizational development. When using an organizational assessment with grantees, three ingredients are critical to success: (1) recognition that all organizations are different and that each situation should be handled with care; (2) respect for the organization's life stage because different life stages represent different challenges; and (3) flexibility because things change and it is rather arrogant to pretend to know what will happen in eighteen months or three years.

PART TWO

Assessing Funder Capacity

A growing number of grantmakers realize that focusing on grantee capacity alone is not enough to leverage resources for the greatest possible impact. Grantmakers must also turn the mirror toward themselves and look critically at their own capacity. Grantmakers who ask grantees to make capacity improvements without being committed to strengthening their own capacity are like the parents who, with cigarettes in hand, warn their children not to smoke.

This section describes the efforts of two philanthropic support organizations—the Center for Effective Philanthropy and the Women's Funding Network—to assess grantmaker capacity through two different lenses. One tool looks at grantmaker effectiveness through the eyes of grantees; the other assesses organizational life-cycle stages as an indication of common capacity challenges.

CHAPTER 5

Turning the Tables on Assessment: The Grantee Perception Report®

by Phil Buchanan, Kevin Bolduc, and Judy Huang,
The Center for Effective Philanthropy

In February 2004, the William and Flora Hewlett Foundation posted on its web site results of a survey that compared the perspectives of Hewlett's grantees on the foundation to the views of grantees of twenty-eight other foundations. Much of the news was positive—showing, for example, that Hewlett was regarded as a leader in its fields of funding to a greater degree than was typical of other foundations whose grantees had been surveyed.

But there was sobering news as well. Areas receiving poorer relative ratings included clarity of communication of foundation goals and strategies and a selection process that, though designed to help push grantees to clarify their own thinking, was regarded as comparatively unhelpful. The foundation's president, Paul Brest, drafted a commentary on the results, and their implications, and posted them on the Hewlett web site along with excerpts of the report.[26]

---

[26] The authors would like to note that the Hewlett Foundation became a funder of the Center for Effective Philanthropy in July 2004 (six months after receiving its Grantee Perception Report). Paul Brest has served as a member of the Center's Advisory Board since 2002 and as a member of the Center's Foundation Performance Metrics Pilot Study Advisory Board. The Center has strict policies with respect to integrity and confidentiality of its data and treats funders and nonfunders equally in the context of its research and provision of assessment tools.

"Much of the Grantee Perception Report was positive," Brest wrote, "but, of course, it was the less positive aspects that got our attention and from which we probably have the most to learn."

This act of self-assessment and disclosure generated significant "buzz" in the foundation sector and led to reports in the *San Jose Mercury News* and the *New York Times,* among other publications. In explaining Hewlett's decision to be public about the survey results, Brest was quoted in the *Times* saying that, given the foundation's concern for strengthening philanthropy, "the more information we can make available, the better we all are."

The *Times* article went on to describe a dynamic between grantees and foundations in which "organizations, which typically live hand to mouth, are understandably wary of alienating any source of financial support." But, the article asserted, "this code of silence is increasingly being challenged." [27]

That the simple acts of surveying grantees, viewing results comparatively, and making the results public would be deemed worthy of widespread discussion in the foundation field—much less mainstream media coverage—speaks volumes both about the state of performance assessment in the foundation field and, perhaps, the increasing scrutiny foundations face. This chapter will

Chapter Overview

The Center for Effective Philanthropy, initially funded in 2001, focuses on providing management and governance tools to define, assess, and improve overall foundation performance. Beginning with a pilot study in 2001, Center staff created the Grantee Perception Report (GPR)—a detailed report of grantee perceptions of various dimensions of foundation performance, portrayed on a *comparative* basis to grantee perceptions of other foundations. This chapter will discuss the origins and future potential of the GPR, including

• Assessing foundation performance

• Challenges in collecting and understanding grantee perceptions
• The power of comparative data
• A new data set and new insights for the field
• Lessons learned
• Reflections on the GPR

The CD-ROM that accompanies this book includes a copy of *Listening to Grantees: What Nonprofits Value in Their Foundation Funders.*

---

[27] Stephanie Strom, "Charities Surprise Donor Foundations With Bluntness," *New York Times,* April 23, 2004.

explore these issues through the story of the development of the tool Hewlett used to gain these insights on its performance.

What Hewlett made public was an excerpt of a Grantee Perception Report (GPR)[28] prepared by the Center for Effective Philanthropy—a nonprofit organization that received initial funding in 2001 and is focused on providing management and governance tools to define, assess, and improve overall foundation performance. The GPR is a detailed report of grantee perceptions of various dimensions of foundation performance, portrayed on a *comparative* basis to grantee perceptions of other foundations. The report covers a range of issues—from perceptions of foundation impact on its fields and communities of funding, to responsiveness and approachability, to quantity and quality of assistance beyond the grant check provided to grantees.

In these pages, the three of us, who have overseen the creation and implementation of the GPR, will discuss its origins and future potential.[29] We will describe the forces that make performance assessment in the foundation field so difficult as well as those that have led to widespread adoption of this tool in a short time-frame. We will illustrate some lessons learned by foundations that have subscribed to the GPR and provide examples of changes made as a result of these new understandings of foundation performance. We will also describe some of the broadly applicable insights gained from the large-scale surveys of grantees we have conducted.

The story of the GPR is one of widespread and rapid adoption of a new assessment tool that has proven to be useful at the board, senior staff, and program staff levels. The GPR has revealed important new information for foundations about clarity of strategy and goals, consistency in process and approach,

---

[28] For more information about the Grantee Perception Report® and links to excerpts and full results of reports that have been made public by individual foundation subscribers, see the web site http://www.effectivephilanthropy.org/assessment/assessment_gpr.html

[29] Phil Buchanan, the Center's first executive director, was the Center's first full-time employee after it received initial funding in summer 2001. Kevin Bolduc, associate director, joined the Center in October 2001, and Judy Huang, senior research analyst, joined the Center in September 2002. The authors wish to acknowledge and thank in particular the following Center staff for their contributions to the work described here: Ellie Buteau, Ellie Carothers, and John Davidson. The Center's founders, Mark Kramer and Michael Porter, and members of the Center's board of directors and advisory board also contributed to this work. See http://www.effectivephilanthropy.org for complete lists of members. Thanks in particular to board members Phil Giudice and Ricardo A. Millett for their comments on an earlier version of this chapter. Finally, this chapter is informed significantly by the insights of GPR subscribers.

usefulness of nonmonetary assistance provided, helpfulness of selection and evaluation processes, and intensity of administrative requirements relative to dollars awarded. This new information has led foundations to recognize and build on strengths, redress weaknesses, and even confront difficult questions of individual program officer performance.

Assessing Foundation Performance

Most leaders in the public, private, and nonprofit sectors believe that assessing performance is a critically important management activity. Assessment provides the basis for learning and improvement, informs future planning, and sheds light on both organizational and individual performance.

Yet even in the corporate world, where assessment would seem straightforward enough, given the availability of commonly understood quantifiable metrics such as profitability, return on investment, and market share, companies routinely struggle for the right set of measures to monitor. The challenge is to find measures that can be tracked in a timely way, are easily understood and acted on within the organization, and are closely connected to achievement of key organizational objectives.

If performance assessment is difficult even in the corporate sector, it often appears harder in the world of mission-driven nonprofit organizations, as many scholars have noted and as other authors in this book discuss. Organizational goals frequently seem not to lend themselves easily to quantification, the language and tradition of assessment is less developed, and management resources are often stretched—consumed by core mission-related work, with little time left for reflection, much less assessment.

But nonprofit organizations face external pressures, such as fundraising or competition from other nonprofit or for-profit enterprises, and these performance pressures typically catalyze and provide some basis for assessment. College and university leaders, for example, routinely consult comparative data on their institutions' appeal among prospective students and on a variety of aspects of institutional performance, from graduation rates to fundraising success to student satisfaction surveys. Leaders of social service agencies can track numbers of clients served and monitor their progress following an intervention, and assess a range of measures of financial and organizational health.

Foundation leaders typically have not had such well-defined measures to rely on. Although foundations often demand that nonprofit grantees assess their performance, they have frequently struggled with assessment of their own performance. The challenge is made tougher by foundations' unique position in society as tax-advantaged organizations shielded from competitive pressures. How do foundations, which seek to affect change primarily through others (their grantees) assess their performance? In the absence of competitive or market pressures of any kind, or significant external pressure, how can performance be assessed?[30] To quote Joel Fleishman of Duke University (and formerly of the Atlantic Philanthropies), "Foundations insist that grant-receiving nonprofits be accountable to them, but to whom are the foundations themselves accountable? To no one but their board, the IRS, and the state attorney general, none of which does, as a general rule, an acceptable job of accountability enforcement."[31]

The story of the Center for Effective Philanthropy's Grantee Perception Report begins with efforts to help advance the discussion of this difficult topic of foundation performance assessment. We were focused, in essence, on a deceptively simple question that many foundation CEOs and board members have asked themselves and their colleagues: *How are we doing?*[32]

The Center for Effective Philanthropy's founding board members, and in particular Phil Giudice, Mark Kramer, and Michael Porter, were convinced that the foundation field could do more to assess and improve its performance. Three foundations stepped forward in 2001 with a total of $345,000 to support the Foundation Performance Metrics Pilot Study: the Atlantic Philanthropies, the Surdna Foundation, and the David and Lucile Packard Foundation.

[30] It is worth acknowledging that community foundations face a fundraising imperative and are therefore not as immune from competitive dynamics as private foundations.

[31] Joel Fleishman, a member of the Center's board of directors, in a speech at the Center's November 2002 seminar "Assessing Foundation Performance: Current Practices, Future Possibilities." For a report on this seminar, see http://www.effectivephilanthropy.org/seminars/seminars_past.html.

[32] For the story of one foundation's efforts to answer this question, see Phil Giudice and Kevin Bolduc, *Assessing Performance at the Robert Wood Johnson Foundation: A Case Study* (Cambridge, MA: Center for Effective Philanthropy, 2004). The report can be downloaded at http://www.effectivephilanthropy.org/publications/publications_overview.html. All Center for Effective Philanthropy publications are available free for download.

The Center set out, first, to understand current practice in performance assessment. We interviewed eighteen CEOs of large, private foundations and fifty-six others, including trustees, senior executives, grantees, and experts in foundation and nonprofit management. We learned that most foundations shared a desire to understand their ultimate social impact, preferably relative to the resources invested. Conceptually, this approach is clear, and could theoretically be achieved by aggregating the social impact of all grants made by the foundation, quantifying and monetizing that impact in some standard way, and viewing the impact relative to total foundation spending.

As a practical matter, however, this is admittedly difficult—if not impossible—at least for the vast majority of large foundations that make dozens or hundreds of grants across multiple program areas, with each grant typically comprising a relatively small proportion of grantees' budgets.[33] Many of the country's largest foundations have significant evaluation budgets, but while evaluations can be very useful in assessing specific grants, grantees, or programs, they suffer from a number of limitations when viewed in the context of overall foundation performance assessment.[34]

A number of CEOs expressed frustration with the utility of the data that results from traditional evaluations in understanding overall foundation performance: in an interview with us, one CEO called such data "so hyper-specific as to be meaningless." Michael Bailin, president of the Edna McConnell Clark Foundation, describes the backward-looking nature of evaluation efforts as "postmortem" and "more of an autopsy than a checkup on a living patient."[35] Others have noted that assessment activities by foundations are typically targeted at grantees, rather than at the performance of the foundations themselves. A 1999 Colorado Trust report put it this way: "Foundations most often

---

[33] Over four rounds of the Center's grantee surveys in 2003 and 2004, encompassing grantees of 117 foundations, the median proportion of a grantee organization's operating budget funded by a given foundation annually was about 3 percent.

[34] See the reports *Toward a Common Language: Listening to Foundation CEOs and Other Experts Talk About Performance Measurement in Philanthropy* (Cambridge, MA: Center for Effective Philanthropy, 2002); and *Indicators of Effectiveness: Understanding and Improving Foundation Performance* (Cambridge, MA: Center for Effective Philanthropy, 2002) at http://www.effective-philanthropy.org/seminars/seminars_past.html.

[35] Michael Bailin, "Re-Engineering Philanthropy: Field Notes From the Trenches," presentation at the Waldemar A. Nielsen Issues in Philanthropy Seminar Series at Georgetown University, February 21, 2003. For full text, go to http://cpnl.georgetown.edu/doc_pool/Nielsen0207Bailin.pdf.

direct their evaluations at the activities of their grantees, only rarely subjecting themselves to the same level of scrutiny, accountability, and discomfort." [36]

We found that, for some foundations, the search for the perfect performance measure appeared to have become the enemy of the good or, indeed, of any measure at all. Some interviewees conceded that, in the absence of unassailable impact measures, what was left was simply a void: little data was routinely accessed by foundation leaders to understand performance. At the board level, the understandable tendency was to focus on that which was easily quantified and compared: investment performance and administrative cost ratios. For example, in a 2002 survey of foundation CEOs the Center conducted, 76 percent described their boards as "substantially involved" in assessing the endowment investment performance of the foundation; just 20 percent said their boards were "substantially involved" in assessing the foundation's social impact.[37]

With this reality as backdrop, we sought to understand what additional data foundation leaders believed would be useful even if the data were more in the category of "indicators of effectiveness" than definitive proof of impact achieved. We created a performance assessment framework (see Figure 6, page 138) and published in our report, *Indicators of Effectiveness: Understanding and Improving Foundation Performance.* Based on what we heard in our interviews, we divided seventeen key measurement topics into four broad categories: Achieving Impact, Setting the Agenda, Managing Operations, and Optimizing Governance.[38] It is the Center for Effective Philanthropy's goal to develop data that informs measurement in these areas as fully as possible.[39]

---

[36] Doug Easterling and Nancy Baughman Csuti, *Using Evaluation to Improve Grantmaking: What's Good for the Goose is Good for the Grantor* (Denver: Colorado Trust, 1999).

[37] See *Indicators of Effectiveness,* 5.

[38] Ibid., 13.

[39] For example, to assist in assessment within the category of "Optimizing Governance" the Center launched the Foundation Governance Project in 2003. That project seeks to develop data that will be useful in informing best practice in foundation governance. The Center is currently planning a research initiative focusing on the category of "Setting the Agenda," with a particular emphasis on program strategy development.

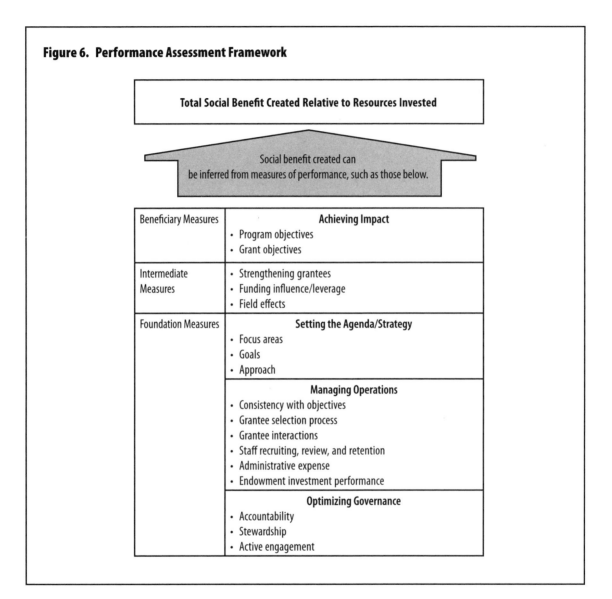

Figure 6. Performance Assessment Framework

Total Social Benefit Created Relative to Resources Invested

Social benefit created can be inferred from measures of performance, such as those below.

Beneficiary Measures	**Achieving Impact** • Program objectives • Grant objectives
Intermediate Measures	• Strengthening grantees • Funding influence/leverage • Field effects
Foundation Measures	**Setting the Agenda/Strategy** • Focus areas • Goals • Approach
	Managing Operations • Consistency with objectives • Grantee selection process • Grantee interactions • Staff recruiting, review, and retention • Administrative expense • Endowment investment performance
	Optimizing Governance • Accountability • Stewardship • Active engagement

For each of the seventeen measurement topics, we identified potential data sources (or indicators of effectiveness) that foundation leaders could draw on. For a number of the specific measures, *grantee perceptions* of foundation performance were one useful potential indicator among many. After all, grantees were being funded by foundations in order to achieve foundation objectives, giving them unique insight into the foundation's performance. Questions for which grantee perceptions were potentially relevant included

- Are we improving grantee effectiveness?
- Do we influence others to fund our grantees?
- Is our selection process clear and uniformly implemented?
- Are we responsive to our grantees and do we treat them fairly?
- Are we seen by grantees to be making a significant positive impact on their fields? Their communities? Their organizations? [40]

The Challenge of Collecting and Understanding Grantee Perceptions

Many examples exist of foundations that have surveyed their grantees through individual customized surveys. But most foundations that survey their grantees receive overwhelmingly positive news. Quantifiable grantee ratings of their foundations cluster toward the high end of an absolute scale and among the open-ended, qualitative comments, the positive statements outnumber the negative. Despite the tendency among many in the field to invoke the analogy of customer satisfaction, surveying grantees proves simply not to be akin to surveying customers in a business setting. After all, customers pay for a service. Grantees, on the other hand, receive money. As some with whom we have discussed this research have suggested, you can only rate a benefactor so low.

As we noted in one of our reports on our Foundation Performance Metrics Pilot Study:

> . . . Several foundations use periodic surveys to probe grantees' perceptions of whether and how the foundation has strengthened grantee performance. Serious questions were raised, however, about the candor and usefulness of grantee responses absent a larger context in which to interpret them. One CEO noted that his foundation had scored highly in a survey of grantees but, in the final analysis, he didn't know what to make of the results. What was an average

---

[40] *Indicators of Effectiveness*, 13.

score? How candid were the grantees given that they were evaluating a crucial source of funding?. . . . [A] need was expressed for better ways of collecting comparative and reliable data that would allow foundations to understand how their own performance had affected their grantees.[41]

Essentially two issues complicated efforts by individual foundations to survey their grantees. First, no matter how many assurances were made by foundations and third-party surveyors regarding confidentiality of responses, foundation executives worried that they were not receiving candid responses from grantees. Second, a lack of comparative data made results difficult to interpret, particularly given that grantee ratings of foundations tended toward the high end of any absolute scales.

Given these issues, we began to explore the possibility of viewing grantee perceptions of foundations on a relative, or comparative, basis. We believed the Center for Effective Philanthropy could establish itself as a trusted, independent collector of candid grantee perspectives and that we could then analyze and present results to individual foundations. We discussed a variety of possibilities for implementing this concept, including asking grantees that had received funding from a variety of foundations to rank or order those foundations on a number of different dimensions.

Ultimately, we chose instead to survey individual foundations' grantees, asking them to rate their experiences with one foundation only. This allowed us to understand in some considerable level of detail both how a foundation's grantees perceived it on many dimensions *as well as how those perceptions compared to how other foundations were perceived by their grantees.* (See Figure 7, Grantee Perception Data, page 141.)

We developed a survey instrument with input from members of our Foundation Performance Metrics Pilot Study advisory board, board of directors, and external experts in survey design. We then tested the instrument with a set of grantee volunteers. Our pilot survey, conducted in 2002, focused on grantees of twenty-three large private foundations that we believed to be representative of the largest one hundred foundations on a number of key dimensions.

---

[41] *Toward a Common Language*, 6.

Figure 7. Grantee Perception Data

Figure 7 shows how comparative grantee perception data increases understanding. On the question of responsiveness, average ratings of foundations by grantees cluster toward the high end of the 1–7 scale. Foundation X might view its results as quite positive if they were presented without an understanding of how other foundations are rated on this dimension—as denoted by the gray line in the left table. However, once results for a set of foundations are displayed (shown by the black lines), it is clear that Foundation X is among the lowest rated. We can say with a high level of statistical certainty that Foundation X is below average on this rating—even though the absolute score is high.

Foundation X Views Grantee Ratings of Staff Responsiveness . . . Comparative Grantee Data Reveals Problems

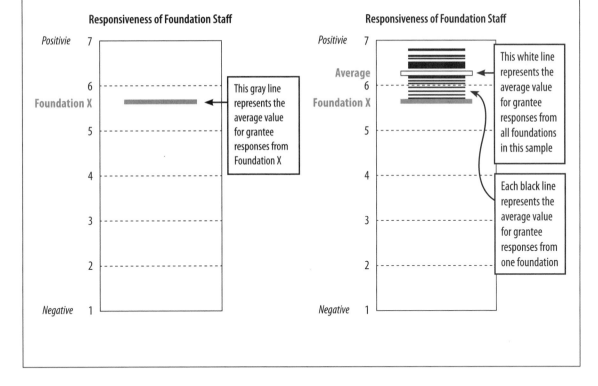

Although most members of our advisory board were supportive, many others with whom we discussed the survey expressed skepticism as to its utility, and some even questioned whether grantee perceptions were relevant at all to issues of foundation effectiveness. As one senior executive at a large, national foundation told us, "Grantees are just a means to our ends. We're not interested in their perspectives." We argued that, given that grantees were the foundation's chosen agents of change, their views on the ways the foundation helped or hindered them were highly relevant to the foundation's ability to achieve its ends. But for this individual, and for some in the field, this argument was not persuasive.

In light of this skepticism, we feared that few foundations would opt into a pilot grantee survey. So we decided to survey grantees of the selected foundations entirely independently. We informed the foundations of our plan to survey their grantees, but we did not rely on their cooperation. Instead, we gleaned grantee contact data from public tax filings of the selected foundations and simply proceeded to survey their grantees. Reactions, not surprisingly, were something less than uniformly positive, with some foundations expressing considerable dismay that we would unilaterally survey "*their*" grantees.

Ultimately, however, more than half of the foundations whose grantees we surveyed during the pilot expressed interest in seeing the results, and we presented some of the data to the senior leadership of those foundations, who found it revealing and useful. This experience taught us that there was, indeed, significant utility in comparative grantee perception data.

The Power of Comparative Data

With the lessons of the pilot effort still fresh, we set out to redesign the survey instrument based on the feedback we received. We created a prototype performance assessment tool for individual foundations that we called the Grantee Perception Report (GPR).[42] In 2003 and 2004, in four discrete rounds, we surveyed more than 22,000 grantees of 117 foundations (most among the largest several hundred in the country), and received nearly 14,000 completed

---

[42] The price of the GPR ranges from under $10,000 to more than $30,000, depending on asset size of the foundation, number of grantees, and degree of customization of our analyses.

responses.[43] Nearly half of those foundations opted into the survey process in order to receive a GPR. The other foundations were surveyed independently to ensure a representative and diverse comparative cohort.[44]

Recognizing that grantees might be reticent or fearful to comment on their funders given their dependence on foundation funding, our processes ensure total confidentiality of individual grantee responses, even allowing grantees the option of responding anonymously. Grantees have been overwhelmingly appreciative of the opportunity to provide this candid and confidential feedback—sometimes noting what a welcome change it is to be asked to "turn the tables" and comment on the performance of their funders.

We have seen that ratings of foundations do still skew toward the high end of an absolute scale, but in comparing foundation averages to one another, there are indeed statistically significant differences. Moreover, the difference in tenor of open-ended comments between a grantee rating a foundation a 4 on a scale of 1 to 7 on a dimension such as satisfaction, for example, and a grantee rating a foundation a 7, is striking. For example, a typical grantee comment when rating a foundation a 7 is: "From the outset of our grant application process, and in ongoing communication with foundation staff, [we] have encountered a cordial, responsive, experienced and highly professional team." A grantee rating a foundation a 4, on the other hand, might use language like this: "The foundation has little appreciation for the burden and unrealistic time demands and deadlines that they impose. They seem to feel we have nothing else to do but respond to them."[45]

The statistically meaningful differences that exist when comparing foundations' average ratings allow for new insights into performance. The existence of such variation has made the GPR a highly valued assessment tool by trustees,

---

[43] Overall response rate was 53 percent in spring 2003 survey round, 66 percent in fall 2003 round, 65 percent in spring 2004 survey round, and 64 percent in fall 2004 survey round.

[44] A number of foundations that were surveyed independently ultimately elected to receive a GPR, bringing the total number of GPR subscribers in 2003 and 2004 to sixty-five. The rapid rate of adoption of the GPR surprised us and stretched the resources of our small, young nonprofit organization. Initially, we observed that GPR subscribers were disproportionately foundations whose leaders knew us through attendance at our seminars or other direct interactions. But the group quickly broadened, particularly as increased media and lawmaker scrutiny of foundations led more foundations to ask themselves whether they were doing all that was necessary to assess and improve their performance.

[45] Actual grantee comments from spring 2004 survey round.

CEOs, senior staff, and program officers. Many foundations that previously believed themselves to have comparatively strong and productive relationships with their grantees have awoken to a different—and sobering—reality.

GPR results cover a wide range of issues from highly subjective perceptions of a foundation's impact on its fields or communities of focus to questions about whether grantees received certain types of assistance beyond the grant check and how much they valued that assistance. They also cover administrative processes from selection to evaluation and reporting. Some foundations, drawing on data provided by the Center, have been able to persuasively demonstrate to their boards that they are seen to be performing comparatively well in these areas. Others have learned that they are doing less well than they had hoped in areas of importance to them, and have therefore reconsidered strategies, policies, and practices.[46]

Some examples of how foundations have used the GPR follow.

- The board and staff of a large private foundation were surprised to find significant concerns among grantees and lower than average ratings on a number of dimensions (such as responsiveness and fairness) that had long been seen as important values by the foundation. The CEO noted in a recent letter to the foundation's grantees that the foundation's past efforts to assess performance had lacked comparative data and that participation in the Center's Grantee Perception Report process shed new light on areas requiring improvement. "The . . . findings were sobering, to put it mildly," the CEO wrote, "suggesting far from optimal performance when compared with some of our peer foundations." The CEO detailed the findings and noted that "we have started to make improvements in the processes that are fundamental to building better and more collaborative relationships with our grantees and colleagues" and begun a "top-to-bottom" reexamination of those processes. "You should begin to see . . . beneficial changes almost immediately," the letter concluded.

- A community foundation saw that it was making repeated one-year small grants to the same organizations, which required significant administrative time for grantees. This frustrated grantees who were looking to program

---

[46] A number of foundations have asked us to survey declined applicants as well. We created a separate survey instrument and corresponding report, the Applicant Perception Report (APR). To date, eleven foundations have commissioned the APR.

officers for leadership on key community issues. And it frustrated program officers who believed the refusal of the foundation's board to consider making fewer, larger grants was hindering their ability to be effective and creating pointlessly high transaction costs for grantees and for them. The foundation is now making fewer, but larger grants and redefining the program officer role to address crucial community needs.

- SC Ministry Foundation in Cincinnati learned that it was highly rated by its grantees on dimensions such as overall satisfaction, responsiveness, approachability, and fairness, and was providing a relatively high level of assistance beyond the grant check.[47] However, the foundation's leaders also learned that the foundation rated comparatively lower in perceived impact on its grantees' fields and influence on public policy. They were also concerned to see that their grants were quite small relative to the administrative requirements placed on grantees. Their ratio of dollars awarded per grantee hour spent on administrative processes was lower than most other foundations. Open-ended comments from grantees questioned whether the balance between the requirements imposed on them and the level of funding received was appropriate. Following internal discussions with staff and the board, the foundation took a number of steps, which it described in a letter sent to all grantees. "We will be . . . aiming toward proportionality between grant size and levels of effort," the letter stated, going on to say that the foundation "will streamline the progress and evaluation reporting formats."

- Another GPR subscriber's board of directors was planning to cut the foundation's research staff because of concerns regarding its relatively high administrative costs—until it learned that this research was highly valued by grantees and a key component of comparatively high grantee perceptions of the foundation's work. The board decided against the cuts.

- The George Gund Foundation in Cleveland, which reported in its 2003 annual report on its largely positive GPR results, learned that one of its program areas "had become an unsatisfactory catch-all. . . . The discernment of our grantees, combined with the need to prioritize economic development, led the foundation to conclude that civic affairs was no longer supportable as a stand-alone program area."[48] The program area was eliminated.

[47] SC Ministry Foundation leaders gave us permission to discuss their confidential GPR results.
[48] George Gund Foundation Annual Report, 2003.

Many foundation GPR subscribers that had previous experience with grantee surveys now realized that in the absence of comparative data, their past efforts to survey their grantees had been limited in value. Frequently, foundations ask us to customize their comparative cohort, in order to see results relative, for example, to other community foundations, other health-focused foundations, or other large national funders. Other foundations are satisfied to see their results against the broad group of foundations whose grantees the Center has surveyed. Regardless of how the comparison is structured, it is the comparative data that makes the GPR valuable.

As the *New York Times* reported in its story on GPR subscribers:

> Foundation executives say one . . . beneficial aspect [of the GPR] was the survey's ability to show how they compared with peers, something they are unable to learn with their own studies. The Greater Cincinnati Foundation had surveyed its own recipients but was disappointed in the results.
>
> "Even though we provided a means for them to talk anonymously, we didn't learn anything, in part because we had nothing to compare the results against," Kathryn Merchant,[49] the foundation's president and chief executive, said.
>
> [After receiving its GPR] the foundation was taken aback to learn that it was the slowest to approve grants of all foundations [whose grantees were surveyed in one of the Center's survey rounds]. So it streamlined reviews of organizations that were seeking grants of $10,000 or less.
>
> "It's not all that scary to get feedback," Ms. Merchant said. "I knew we were going to get slammed on the time thing, but getting the information that compared us to others really helped us change practices that had been around a long time."[50]

---

[49] Merchant is a member of the Center's Advisory Board.

[50] Stephanie Strom, "Charities Surprise Donor Foundations With Bluntness," *New York Times,* April 23, 2004.

Comparative data by program area and program officer

Beyond illustrating average ratings of a foundation relative to grantee ratings of other foundations, the GPR allows for comparison among program areas or program officers. Increasingly, GPR subscribers have mined this data extensively to understand the strengths and weaknesses of individual program areas and/or program officers. We have found that, at many foundations, the differences in grantee perceptions among program areas and/or program officers are as great as the difference among foundations.

Sometimes, the results have uncovered significant performance issues in the form of deep concern among grantees about a particular program officer's unresponsiveness or arrogance. In other cases, the program area or program officer level data has simply facilitated productive discussions about whether differences in program officers' behavior with grantees are intentional and make sense in light of differences in program goals—or whether they are unintentional and therefore potentially more problematic. Some program level data has highlighted for foundations significant areas of leadership and expertise previously not well recognized.

A New Data Set and New Insights for the Field

Beyond allowing individual foundations to obtain valuable data on their performance, the grantee survey process has allowed the Center to develop a rich new data set from which we can distill lessons of broad relevance to those in the field. Through the data, we were able to dispel some myths.

For example, some believed that our grantee survey efforts would prove pointless because grantee perceptions would be systematically skewed by forces that had little to do with foundation leadership. Maybe, for example, grantees' ratings of a foundation would be based largely on the size of the grant they received: the bigger the grant, the higher the ratings. Our analysis of the data demonstrated that this is not the case. It turns out that structural characteristics of the grant, grantee, or foundation are not key predictors of grantee perceptions. Grant size or type, grantee size or focus, or foundation size or type do not explain much of the variation that exists in grantee perceptions.

It is instead other attributes related to staff conduct and expertise—attributes achievable within a variety of foundation structures—that predict grantee ratings of satisfaction with their funders, impact on the grantee organization, impact on the community, and impact on the field. This is a crucial finding that is explored in our paper, *Listening to Grantees: What Nonprofits Value in their Foundation Funders,* which analyzes our spring 2003 survey results.

Sample Grantee Survey Questions

A. Overall, how would you rate the Foundation's impact on your field?

1	2	3	4	5	6	7
No impact						Significant positive impact

B. How well does the Foundation understand the local community in which you operate?

1	2	3	4	5	6	7
Limited understanding of the community						Regarded as an expert on the community

C. How helpful to you was participating in the Foundation's selection process in strengthening your program/organization?

1	2	3	4	5	6	7
Not at all helpful						Extremely helpful

D. Overall, how fairly did the Foundation treat you?

1	2	3	4	5	6	7
Not at all fairly						Extremely fairly

E. What improvements would you suggest in the Foundation's services or processes that would make them a better funder?

(A copy of this paper is included on the CD-ROM that accompanies this book.) In a forthcoming paper, we will offer further analyses of a combined data set of several rounds of grantee surveys. (See sidebar, What Nonprofits Value in Their Foundation Funders, page 150.)

Our analysis indicates that the attributes that most foundation leaders use to describe their foundations—attributes such as size and program focus—do not explain differences in grantee perceptions of overall dimensions such as satisfaction and impact. Put another way, our analysis belies the adage that "when you've seen one foundation, you've seen one foundation." It reveals, instead, that there are common characteristics of foundations that have strong relationships with grantees and that these characteristics cut across the attributes that many in the field believe define differences among foundations.

The grantee survey process has also allowed us to inform the field about the range of foundation practices on basic process dimensions such as grant turnaround, time required of grantees during the selection and evaluation processes, or data requested by foundations during those processes. There is, for example, a wide range of foundation averages in the length of the selection process. Of the thirty foundations in our spring 2003 survey, for example, the average time from submission of a grant request to receipt of funds was 5.7 months, but one foundation took an average of more than a year. Similar variation exists in the administrative burdens placed on grantees, with some foundations providing an average of less than $1,000 per hour required of grantees on administrative processes such as selection and reporting, and others providing as much as $8,000 per hour.

Lessons Learned

The stories that emerge from the GPR experience are diverse and varied, as the examples we have described make clear. But, with the benefit of having delivered more than fifty of these reports over the past two years, a number of lessons have emerged:

- GPR data is relevant at the program officer, senior management, and board levels.

What Nonprofits Value in Their Foundation Funders

The relationship between foundations and grantees is much discussed, debated, and dissected. Competing theories abound regarding the key attributes of successful and satisfying foundation-grantee relations: most are informed by speculation about what nonprofits really value. What is often missing from these discussions, however, is rigorously collected and large-scale data about the opinions of grantees.[51]

In *Listening to Grantees: What Nonprofits Value in Their Foundation Funders,* we sought to go beyond looking at comparisons of individual foundation grantee perception data and address findings more globally through analysis of our spring 2003 survey round, which included 3,184 grantees of thirty foundations. We identified three factors—which we refer to as the three dimensions of foundation performance that grantees value in their foundation funders—that best predict variation in overall grantee satisfaction. They are

1. Quality of interactions with foundation staff: fairness, responsiveness, approachability.

2. Clarity of communications of a foundation's goals and strategy: clear and consistent articulation of objectives.

3. Expertise and external orientation of the foundation: understanding of fields and communities of funding and ability to advance knowledge and affect public policy.

These dimensions, and their implications for foundation leaders, are explored in detail in *Listening to Grantees.* Specific implications include making necessary investments to perform well on the three dimensions; supporting the development of specific and relevant expertise by program officers and foundation staff; aligning operations to optimize grantmaking patterns or policies that increase program officer ability to concentrate on the three dimensions; seeking to maintain consistent focus and direction ensuring consistency of policy and communication; communicating frequently; providing timely feedback to grantees; and seeking confidential, comparative feedback from grantees.

Typically, we present GPR results to foundation program staff, senior staff, and boards, often in several separate meetings. The GPR has relevant information at each of these levels. To grantees, the foundation is the program officer, and perspectives on the foundation relate directly to perspectives on the particular program officer(s) with whom they interact.[52] But, as we noted in *Listening to Grantees,* "many of the implications [of the data] cannot be

---

[51] Excerpted from the Executive Summary of Phil Buchanan, Kevin Bolduc, and Judy Huang, *Listening to Grantees: What Nonprofits Value in Their Foundation Funders* (Cambridge, MA: Center for Effective Philanthropy, 2004), 2.

[52] See ibid. Also, in her 1999 focus groups with grantees for the Forum of Regional Associations of Grantmakers, Marcia Sharp drew a similar conclusion, noting in her report that "For grantees thinking about particular foundations, as opposed to the overall group, it is clear that 'the program officer is the foundation.'"

acted on by program officers in isolation. Indeed, to undertake the key activities necessary for strong relationships with grantees, resources need to be aligned and job descriptions crafted in a way that allows the program officer to do what is needed." [53]

- Results must be viewed in the context of a foundation's strategy and values.

An understandable initial reaction of foundations that receive their GPR results is to focus on all dimensions on which the foundation is perceived less positively on a rating scale than others whose grantees we surveyed. But it is important to remember that being the highest rated on a particular dimension isn't always appropriate, given a foundation's strategy or priorities. For example, foundations that do not seek to influence public policy should take heart—rather than despair—when their grantees rate their impact on public policy to be comparatively minimal. Almost every foundation has areas of relative strengths and relative weakness, and, in the best cases, those correspond to the foundation's priorities and theory of change.

- Strong leadership is required to identify priorities in responding to results of concern.

For foundations that receive disappointing ratings from grantees across a range of dimensions of importance to the foundation, responding effectively can be difficult. The natural tendency is to seek to deny the results by explaining them away as the result of some specific, unusual circumstance, such as staff transitions, or even to question whether grantee perspectives are important or legitimate. We have seen strong leadership overcome this kind of initial reaction. Several keys to success are

- Involving staff in designing solutions to the problem, ensuring that they feel a sense of ownership and responsibility for the process

- Mobilizing foundation staff around some early, "easy wins," such as a redesign of an inefficient process, in order to generate momentum, confidence, and enthusiasm

- Communicating clearly throughout the organization the relative priorities and sequencing of action steps

[53] Ibid., 17.

- Communication back to grantees regarding what was learned through the process is crucial, and generates significant goodwill.

  If grantees are to change their views of a foundation, they need to know that the foundation has taken their feedback to heart. We have been struck by how seriously grantees take our surveys, answering thoughtfully and with eloquent open-ended comments that accompany their numerical ratings. Foundations that have communicated back to grantees in a timely and candid manner have received significant positive responses. Grantees, aware that the GPR results have been delivered and are being acted upon, express support for the foundation's efforts to improve.

- Grantee perceptions are just one perspective on foundation performance.

  As powerful as the GPR has proven to be as an assessment tool, remember that it offers only one perspective on foundation performance. While grantees are undoubtedly crucial partners for foundations as their chosen agents of change, they are not the only constituency with valuable perspectives on a foundation's performance. Policymakers, declined applicants, community leaders, and those served by grantees are just a few of the additional populations that also may have valuable insight into a foundation's effectiveness. Finally, perception data is not the same as hard data on a foundation's ultimate social impact. As we have already discussed, in many cases, it may not be possible to know definitively whether current strategies will yield eventual impact or to develop an exact equation of impact relative to resources invested. But foundation leaders should still do their best to develop as much information as possible to help them understand as fully as possible whether they are achieving their objectives. They should also work to ensure that they have, in each of their areas of programmatic focus, a well-defined strategy, or theory of change, linking activities to desired outcomes. Some, such as Paul Brest of the Hewlett Foundation, have suggested that the ability to articulate this connection between grantmaking and other activities and desired outcomes may be the best proxy of all for foundation effectiveness.

Reflections on the Grantee Perception Report®

The rapid adoption of the GPR has been fueled by a number of different forces: the natural desire of foundation leaders to do the best they can in their work; a sense that it is only fair for foundations to subject themselves to assessment processes given that foundations so often require such processes of their grantees; and heightened scrutiny from the media and lawmakers.

We found early on in our work on performance assessment that significant frustration existed among foundation leaders about the lack of access to data that can inform their efforts to assess performance. Many were drawn to the GPR simply because it offered some way to gauge effectiveness and established baselines in some important areas. They were hungry, in other words, for any kind of feedback that might help them to learn and improve. This is perhaps the most significant force driving interest in the GPR.

A number of leaders in the foundation field are also increasingly uncomfortable with the tendency to translate calls for foundation accountability into increased demands on nonprofits without asking questions about the effectiveness of foundations themselves. The disconnect between what is asked of grantees and what foundations ask of themselves—noted both in Joel Fleishman's talk and in the Colorado Trust report mentioned earlier in the chapter—does not sit well with many foundation leaders. Many leaders in the field have experience as grantees and bring to their positions a desire to avoid the kind of double standard on questions of performance assessment that they believe they sometimes observed while on the other side of the conference room table.

Finally, the heightened scrutiny of foundations from the media and lawmakers over the past several years has undoubtedly also driven interest in the GPR and other Center for Effective Philanthropy initiatives—such as the Foundation Governance Project—as foundations look for ways to demonstrate a commitment to effectiveness, standards, and accountability. Several foundation leaders

Is the Grantee Perception Report® Right for Your Foundation?

Foundations of a wide range of sizes, geographic foci, strategies, and grantmaking priorities have participated in the GPR process. Several questions are helpful in determining if this is an appropriate tool for your foundation.

- *Do you believe that grantees have a valid perspective on the foundation's work, and are you ready to act on their feedback?* If not, there is no purpose served in asking grantees to take the time and energy to participate in the process. Little is accomplished if foundations obtain the GPR without being open to making changes to improve on the basis of what is learned.

- *Do you employ several staff members?* Many of the questions on the GPR survey instrument relate to interactions with, and assistance pro-

vided by, staff. The Center does not recommend the GPR for foundations without staff.

- *Do you have at least thirty grantees?* We believe that this is a threshold number to make surveying worthwhile and to ensure that grantees feel comfortable responding.

If the answer to each of these questions is yes, then contact the Center for Effective Philanthropy to discuss timing, cost, and other logistics. The Center surveys grantees twice a year, once in the spring and once in the fall. The deadline for participation in the spring round is in early January; the deadline for participation in the fall round is early July. The entire process takes approximately six months from the decision to participate to presentation of the GPR.

have expressed a concern that, without a positive story to tell the public, media, and lawmakers—a story that includes specific steps being undertaken to improve performance (not simply to avoid malfeasance)—there is little chance of heightening the esteem in which foundations are held.

One senior executive at a large national foundation, speaking at a gathering of foundation colleagues, described his foundation's decision to obtain the GPR as a direct response to the changed external environment. In so doing, he cited the adage, "When you are going to get run out of town on a rail, get in front and make it look like a parade." And Diana Gurieva, executive vice president of the Dyson Foundation, one of the first foundations to commission a GPR, put it this way: "If we believe there is an important core good in partnering with grantees, then the Grantee Perception Report is a valuable tool to help us be better at it. Also, having a sense of how our grantees perceive us is an important self-critique in light of recent public criticisms of foundations."[54]

---

[54] Diana Gurieva, speaking at the Center's October 2003 seminar on foundation effectiveness.

In keeping with foundation efforts to demonstrate accountability and transparency, an increasing number of foundations are being public not just about their decision to obtain the GPR but, following Hewlett's lead, about their results—posting some or all of the data on their web sites. The Rhode Island Foundation, for example, posted its GPR results and took out an ad in the *Providence Journal* inviting the public to review the report:

> Ask any funding source: Truth is hard to find sometimes. Understandably, people are reluctant to "bite the hands that feeds them." . . . Critics and second opinions are required if an organization wants to grow, improve, and serve its various customers better. Anonymity makes truth-telling and tough love possible. And we're already changing as a result.[55]

It has become a less tenable position to simply throw one's hands in the air and say, "You can't assess this stuff." While it is true that it is very difficult, and perhaps in many cases impossible, to assess a foundation's total social impact precisely, in fact, much can be assessed that reflects on questions of foundation performance and effectiveness. Doing so is important, then, not for its own sake, but because it generates learning, which leads to improvement.

Indeed, the Center's work is guided by the framework for performance assessment laid out in our report *Indicators of Effectiveness* referenced earlier in this chapter. We believe a complete effort to answer the questions outlined in that report represents the best opportunity to understand foundation performance. We are beginning to explore ways to use our various assessment tools in combination as part of a comprehensive assessment of foundation performance that addresses all of the areas outlined in our framework (under the broad headings of Achieving Impact, Setting the Agenda, Managing Operations, and Optimizing Governance). After all, foundations will never have one simple tool by which they can assess their performance in its totality. The nature of foundation work makes assessment a challenge and necessitates a creative approach that taps into multiple data sources to offer a set of "indicators of effectiveness."

---

[55] Rhode Island Foundation, op-ed page advertisement, *Providence Journal*, September 15, 2004, and September 21, 2004.

The Grantee Perception Report (GPR) has proven to be one effective tool, and we are encouraged by the positive changes that are beginning to occur among foundations as a result of bringing the grantee perspective more fully into focus in the context of foundation performance assessment. Grantees have much to say that is crucial for foundations to understand. As one grantee wrote in responding to one of our surveys, "I think it would be helpful if foundations listened more closely to nonprofit organizations as to what it is they need." Grantees will, if asked in a way that ensures confidentiality, provide valuable insight into a foundation's areas of relative strengths and weakness. While they can sometimes be critical, they can also recognize excellence. As one grantee put it, "I work with four foundations. This one is in a class by itself in terms of staff professionalism, respectful treatment of grantees, focus of mission, and creativity. It is a student of excellence in its chosen fields."

Understanding whether grantees believe a foundation is meeting this kind of high standard or falling short can be a crucial component of a larger performance assessment effort. After all, grantees have a unique perspective into the strengths and weaknesses of foundations, but they may feel inhibited in their ability to provide this feedback freely to foundations.

The GPR was created out of recognition of those forces that can impede communication, most significantly the power differential inherent in a relationship between those who have money and those who need it. The GPR, then, is about listening and learning, and enabling foundations to see strengths and weaknesses on a comparative basis. And it is about improving—such that objectives shared by foundations and grantees are more likely to be met, and social good created.

CHAPTER 6

SMART GROWTH:
A Life-Stage Model for
Social Change Philanthropy

by Stephanie Clohesy for The Women's Funding Network

The creation and operation of a foundation is one of the most visionary and idealistic of experiences. Through philanthropy, an individual, a family, or a network of friends and allies invest their own sense of what is good and valuable in the human experience and put it to work to solve problems and help create a better world. Great philanthropic vision aided by great implementation can be exhilarating for donors, deeply satisfying for staff and board, and transformative for beneficiaries and the society. But, on the flip side, great vision ineffectively implemented can be discouraging for donors and even harmful in the community or society.

Effectiveness in philanthropy usually is perceived when a foundation hits a "winner" by funding a person or institution that makes a significant and recognizable difference. But effectiveness has its roots in the foundation's ability to translate vision into exciting but realistic grantmaking strategies and into fundamental capacities that engage the board, build a staff, establish systems, and create culture and trusting relationships.

In 2002 the Women's Funding Network (WFN), an international alliance of more than one hundred public, private, and family foundations led by women and dedicated to achieving full equality and participation of women and girls, proposed to its members that their strategic influence and financial growth are tied to their overall organizational development. As part of this proposition, WFN offered to its member funds a new organizational development tool to assess life-stage advancement and discover the accelerating and inhibiting forces in its core organizational capacities. SMART GROWTH: A Life-Stage Model for Social Change Philanthropy helps member foundations establish a shared understanding of their organization as a way of clarifying problems or challenges and planning for future growth and effectiveness.

This chapter provides a description of SMART GROWTH, including some details of its conceptual evolution that justify its design and approach. Finally, some best practice ideas—discovered during two years of using SMART GROWTH in foundations throughout the world—are shared so that readers can consider the benefits of assessing an organization's life stage to aid in organizational development.

Chapter Overview

In 2002 the Women's Funding Network (WFN) offered to its member funds SMART GROWTH, a new organizational development tool to help them establish a shared understanding of their organization as a way of clarifying problems or challenges and planning for future growth and effectiveness. This chapter will discuss the evolution of SMART GROWTH and will offer some best practice ideas. Topics covered in the text include

- The SMART GROWTH Model
- Development of SMART GROWTH
- Using the tool
- Success stories
- Frequently asked questions
- Lessons learned

The CD-ROM that accompanies this book includes the following materials to support this chapter:

- *Smart Growth Quick Quiz for Private Foundations*
- *Quick Quiz Answer Key for Private Foundations* (the answer key that accompanies the Smart Growth Quiz)
- *The Smart Growth Quick Quiz and Answer Key for Public Foundations*

The SMART GROWTH Model

The SMART GROWTH series of assessment and development tools created by WFN offers a clean and clear model for understanding and practicing good organizational development. Built on a basic matrix of six life stages and twelve functional capacities, SMART GROWTH features the unique, foundation-specific skills of philanthropic organizations such as grantmaking and community convening. SMART GROWTH enables a foundation's staff or board members to describe strengths, find its areas of weakness, and analyze inhibitors and accelerators of effectiveness. SMART GROWTH is especially useful for those funders who are seeking to make a real difference in the world and want to maximize the greatest social benefit through their philanthropy.

Effectiveness comes through a learning process and is not instant or automatic for any organization, including foundations. Tools like SMART GROWTH are primarily for learning. The assessment process gives a "score" to the organization by enabling users to analyze their practices capacity by capacity, thereby determining their organization's life stage. Ideas about how to become more effective emerge through dialogue and the calibration of perspectives among several or many stakeholders who participate in the assessment process.

SMART GROWTH does not produce a strictly mathematical or quantifiable diagnostic conclusion. However, the life-stage score will provide a reliable benchmark from year to year. The life-stage score and corresponding analysis enable the organization to track progress—whether that is movement to a higher life stage or stabilization at a comfortable life stage. Regularly benchmarking an organization also can catch regression in particular capacities.

The SMART GROWTH tool includes

- The Model: six concepts of life stage development
- The Quick Quiz: an online first-step assessment that quickly aggregates results from staff and board
- The Capacity Assessments: a deeper analysis of each of the twelve capacities

- The Resource Materials:
  - An analysis of each capacity and life stage and the inhibitors, accelerators, and best practice tips that are associated with each
  - An annotated reference list that lists other tools and readings, and keys them to SMART GROWTH stages and capacities

- The Success Circle: a shortcut through the twelve capacities to see how they affect the solution to a specific problem

The tools listed above are available in versions for public foundations, private foundations, and individual funds within community foundations.

The six stages are

1. *Envision & Commit:* Founders articulate their vision of a better future, affirm shared values, and explore options for organizational structure.

2. *Start-up & Launch:* High activity by founders results in a formal structure, specific mission, initial funding, basic procedures, and designation of leadership roles. Planning and operations remain informal.

3. *Grow & Deliver:* First spurts of growth and program activity bring formalization of board structure and leadership roles. Sustainability and financial base of the fund need direction and resolution.

4. *Delegate & Evaluate:* Financial and program growth require additional staffing, specialization among staff and between staff and board, and some decentralization of decision making and greater accountability. Demand begins pressuring growth strategies.

5. *Specialize & Control:* Growth and specialization of duties create a proliferation of activities. Management temporarily shifts from decentralization to higher control. Good visibility and good reputation help fuel fundraising along with demands for better proof of outcomes.

6. *Renew & Rebuild:* Changing external and internal forces propel the fund into a major review and renewal of itself. New strategic ideas, new financial plans, new systems—and often new people and roles—are all assimilated as the foundation prepares itself for a new cycle of life.[56]

---

[56] The six stages described here were influenced by the earlier work of Judith Sharken Simon, *The Five Life Stages of Nonprofit Organizations: Where You Are, Where You're Going, and What to Expect When You Get There* (St. Paul, MN: Fieldstone Alliance, 2001).

Foundations move from state to state in a cycle of organizational life. Sometimes organizations move forward smoothly and sequentially from state to state. Other times they move back and forth, surging forward into a new stage, then losing some ground (for example, due to investment losses, departure of staff, and so forth). In these instances, going back to a previous stage may consolidate strengths. Forces that seem to be tugging in opposite directions are usually complementary and part of the growth process in each life stage. Each stage is complex and requires flexibility and ability in both the leadership and the processes. Organizations may move through various cycles in their lifetime.

Figure 8. Six Life Stages of SMART GROWTH (page 162), illustrates the stages.

The twelve capacities are

- Planning
- Programs
- Grantmaking
- Resource development
- Financial management
- Systems
- Marketing and strategic communications
- Staff
- Board/governance
- Values
- Community role
- Impact/measurement[57]

---

[57] SMART GROWTH—PF, designed to address the needs of private and family foundations, includes only eleven capacities because most private foundations do not need the resource development capacity.

Figure 8: Six Life Stages of SMART GROWTH

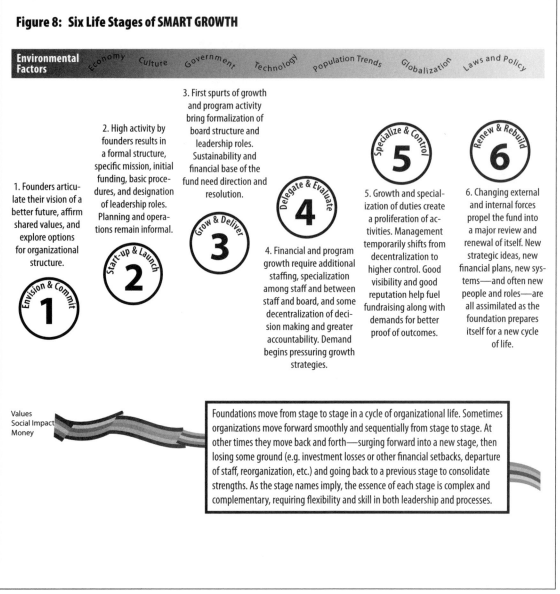

Environmental Factors — Economy · Culture · Government · Technology · Population Trends · Globalization · Laws and Policy

1. Envision & Commit — 1. Founders articulate their vision of a better future, affirm shared values, and explore options for organizational structure.

2. Start-up & Launch — 2. High activity by founders results in a formal structure, specific mission, initial funding, basic procedures, and designation of leadership roles. Planning and operations remain informal.

3. Grow & Deliver — 3. First spurts of growth and program activity bring formalization of board structure and leadership roles. Sustainability and financial base of the fund need direction and resolution.

4. Delegate & Evaluate — 4. Financial and program growth require additional staffing, specialization among staff and between staff and board, and some decentralization of decision making and greater accountability. Demand begins pressuring growth strategies.

5. Specialize & Control — 5. Growth and specialization of duties create a proliferation of activities. Management temporarily shifts from decentralization to higher control. Good visibility and good reputation help fuel fundraising along with demands for better proof of outcomes.

6. Renew & Rebuild — 6. Changing external and internal forces propel the fund into a major review and renewal of itself. New strategic ideas, new financial plans, new systems—and often new people and roles—are all assimilated as the foundation prepares itself for a new cycle of life.

Values · Social Impact · Money

Foundations move from stage to stage in a cycle of organizational life. Sometimes organizations move forward smoothly and sequentially from stage to stage. At other times they move back and forth—surging forward into a new stage, then losing some ground (e.g. investment losses or other financial setbacks, departure of staff, reorganization, etc.) and going back to a previous stage to consolidate strengths. As the stage names imply, the essence of each stage is complex and complementary, requiring flexibility and skill in both leadership and processes.

The Development of SMART GROWTH

The Women's Funding Network initiated the SMART GROWTH project in the belief that its members share similar patterns of development with predictable organizational shifts, growth spurts, and crises. Additionally, WFN was eager to upgrade its capacity to capture the knowledge of its members and to facilitate more of the peer-to-peer learning already highly prized among its members. WFN leaders reasoned that documenting and synthesizing the practical experiences among members in various stages of organizational growth and development would lead women's funds to their own unique "theory" of organizational development. By creating a theory or framework for members' development, WFN would then be able to construct tools and materials to assess and help members achieve organizational progress.

The SMART GROWTH program was conducted through a partnership between WFN and Clohesy Consulting.

The SMART GROWTH team organized their work in 2001–2002 in three major components:

1. Research the field of organizational development, especially life-stage ideas

2. Analyze the real-life development patterns of women's foundations

3. Create a tool to help women's funds in their organizational development process

Benefits of a life-cycle model

A life-cycle model offers leaders a practical metaphor that reduces some of the abstract language of organizational development. Life stages also provide a positive view of forward motion in an organization without locking it into a strictly linear model.

As a life-stage assessment process such as SMART GROWTH begins to yield a stage identity, those in the organization can see that they have clearly moved beyond some early stages of development and can be reassured that the lack of some capacities is due to gradual growth patterns rather than inadequacy.

Some SMART GROWTH scoring also will indicate that an organization is in transition as scores are distributed among two or three adjacent stages. Most organizations will recognize that such transitions mean that an organization may naturally move backward and forward before it ultimately leaps to a new stage of development.

Interviews conducted early in the process of creating SMART GROWTH guided the work toward using a life-cycle model because respondents reacted positively to the concept and became willing to engage in an analytical and nondefensive discussion of their organization. The life-cycle model is easy to grasp, allows room for interpretation, and resonates closely with the ways in which people experience progress (or setbacks) in their organizations.

Research on organizational life cycles

Overall, the seven-month learning process involved intensive interviews with nearly thirty member organizations. In addition, the research team analyzed hundreds of other organizational development tools and resources. The research process identified many existing development tools that have been used by women's foundations. Yet none of the tools discovered during the research process were designed specifically for philanthropic organizations. Effective grantmaking requires strong strategic and conceptual skills, situationally useful levels of engagement, and the ability to match resources to good ideas. Foundations often have unique power to convene others and broker solutions in their community or a field of interest. Therefore the "community role" capacity for a funder also is different than in a typical nonprofit organization.

The SMART GROWTH project team was hopeful that somewhere in the many books and reports about organizational development available in 2001–2002 would be a life-stage model based on philanthropic organizations and reflective of the values-based and participatory style of women's funds. Therefore the literature review on life-cycle theory and models was an important first step in the process. The team set out to understand how other models were developed, compare for-profit and nonprofit models, analyze the models for their value to women's funds, and decide if any of the models could be adopted and adapted by women's funds.

The team discovered that most life-cycle materials share a similar structure. Different organizational factors, such as staffing, product development, innovation, and marketing, define and describe each stage. The stages often are depicted as "organic," meaning the developing organization has within it an underlying form, logic, program, or code that regulates the process of change. Many authors contend that stages are linear in progression and are not easily reversed, though others recognize a continuously changing circle of growth.

Most models also suggest that characteristics present in one stage are continued in some form into the next stage and are, in fact, critical to the progression of the next stage. Most models emphasize that environmental factors (external and internal) may affect or be affected by organizational structure and life cycle.

There are criticisms of the life-stage approach to organizational development, and the SMART GROWTH team considered the criticisms before settling on the life-stage model. Some of the criticisms include

- The "inevitability" of life cycles is too confining and does not adequately encompass environmental factors or the specificity of organizational circumstances

- Life cycles leave too little room for an organization to "regress" or be "stuck" in developmental stages, even though this is a reality at moments in every organization's life

- The model may be too simple for large and complex organizations that may have many of their own departments and teams at various life stages at the same moment

From the organizational development and life-stage research, the SMART GROWTH team concluded that no model existed that could easily be adapted for philanthropic organizations—especially women's funds. However, the research helped the team gain several insights and ideas to build into WFN's new model.

- Life stages are important, but what happens between the stages is equally or even more important. The sense of constant transition in organizations is a familiar one and leaders often exhaust themselves and their staff with a sense of discontent or anxiety over transitions. However, SMART GROWTH's "life between stages" concept enables organizations to see that much of organizational life is lived between stages.

- Life-stage models help to explain the constant and cyclical process of change and reinvention that most organizations experience. Organizations naturally move backward and forward before a definable growth leap occurs. Also, most organizations are generally at one stage while many of their individual parts (teams, special projects, new initiatives, and so forth) are at many stages simultaneously.

- External forces and the changing reality of the outside world need to be incorporated into women's foundations' planning and development. Few—if any—major issues in the economic, social, cultural, or political realm can be solved without taking gender into account. And there are few accomplishments that women's funds can make without considering how to work within the dominant context.

- The importance of individual self-empowerment and autonomy in the creation of social change is a fundamental concept for women's foundations' strategy. Because these values of self-organizing determine both process and results in women's funds, the women's funds are often effective—beyond their size—in accomplishing social change. Some recent examples of this include the leadership role that women's funds took in funding the redefinition of international human rights laws and standards to include women's rights.

- Self-organizing and the engagement of many minds ("hive-mind") help organizations discover truth and innovate. To get an accurate view of the organization's life stage, the assessment tool should engage many people in the process.

Six underlying concepts

The literature search and the foundation-based interviews yielded the basic components of the model now known as the "Smart Growth Model: Six Big Concepts:

- *Big Concept #1: Inside-Out/Outside-In Context Analysis.* As a foundation grows it must build upon three elements of its inner identity—values, social change impact, and money—while being equally aware of the effects the external environment has on the foundation's niche and value.

- *Big Concept #2: Six Life Stages.* A foundation moves back and forth between six stages in a cycle of organizational life.

- *Big Concept #3: Life Stage Leaps.* A foundation moves from stage to stage in an S-shape curve, leaping to a new stage at a peak of momentum without ever experiencing a full decline of momentum on the downside of the curve.

- *Big Concept #4: Life Between Stages.* The transitions between life stages are an integral part of foundation development. Internal and external accelerators and inhibitors influence how a foundation moves between stages.

- *Big Concept #5: Moving to Another Life Cycle.* Once a foundation reaches stage 6 (Renew and Rebuild) it prepares to move through a new life cycle. A foundation reinvents itself by moving again through activities related to earlier stages.

- *Big Concept #6: Twelve Essential Capacities and Skills.* As a foundation moves through the life cycle, it build skills around twelve capacities.

Modifications

A year after the first version of SMART GROWTH was available for WFN's own members, the design team interviewed family foundations and conducted focus groups that ultimately led to the adaptation: SMART GROWTH—PF: A Life Stage Model for Philanthropy. Additionally, women's funds within community foundations have collaborated with the SMART GROWTH team to revise the model for the unique needs of their organizations.

The experiences of donors in the process of creating new foundations also led the team to create SMART GROWTH for Startup Foundations.

Using the Tool

SMART GROWTH was designed to be an easy hands-on tool for "do-it-your-selfers" that would, despite its simplicity, yield rich and complex information to its users. This was done intentionally in response to the executive directors engaged in the SMART GROWTH research who all said resoundingly, "If it is difficult to use . . . if we need to spend days reading the facilitator's manual before we can jump in . . . if it takes too long to get useful information . . . don't even bother creating it!" Some CEOs felt they had little time to devote to organizational assessment; others had few—if any—financial resources for organizational development.

At the same time some foundations interviewed said they already were engaged in serious organizational development and coaching and they wanted a tool that their consultants could interpret and use as part of a larger developmental process. To meet these demands, the SMART GROWTH tool was designed to be flexible. It includes components that can be applied quickly and easily, but it can also be used to provoke deeper discussions about building capacity and to achieve group consensus about what the organization needs. It can be used as a stand-alone or facilitated tool.

Quick and easy

The SMART GROWTH Quick Quiz is a twelve-question online quiz that can be completed in about fifteen minutes and analyzed on the spot to determine an organization's (or department's) overall and approximate life-stage, as well as the life stage of each of its twelve capacities. It can be completed by one person who wants instant insight into the organization's capacity level, by multiple staff, or by board members who are interested in seeing how others view the organization's capacity level. It can also be a useful ice-breaker to engage board members or staff in a discussion about organizational capacity. The online quiz was created to capture and show individual responses as well as the aggregate responses for an organization.

The online quiz is a positive and neutral tool for engaging board and staff to appreciate their different perceptions about the organization and to work with these differences in their plans to strengthen their foundation. User feedback has proven it to be quite accurate in establishing an organization's life stage, making it a valuable first step in the diagnostic process. Findings from the Quick Quiz help the foundation prioritize use of the capacity assessments.

For specific organizational problems, the Smart Growth Success Circle provides a method of focusing on the problem as it relates to each capacity. Using the Success Circle, a problem-solving group can challenge themselves by considering what strengths they need in each capacity to achieve or solve the goal or problem in question. For example, if an organization is considering launching an endowment campaign, they may ask questions such as, What kind of board and governance strength are required for us to launch a successful endowment campaign? What will we need from the board? What kind of staffing will be needed to launch an endowment campaign of the size we envision? What skills do we need? Which people do we need?

By the end of the exercise, a staff group or committee will have a good analysis of the comprehensive mix of capacities needed to carry forward a plan or new goal.

Deep and thoughtful

SMART GROWTH offers an assessment for each of the twelve capacities, which can then be unified to form a composite picture of the organization's life-stage development.

The capacity-by-capacity assessments are a checklist of best practices or common pitfalls stage by stage for each capacity. By checking all the descriptors that apply, users quickly begin to see the primary stage of development as well as secondary levels that may indicate stages behind and ahead. This information can be interpreted to determine whether the organization is firmly rooted in a stage of development or is in transitional activity toward a new stage. Through discussion, users can analyze accelerators and inhibitors, judge the importance of the data, and set some goals.

Assessing and building capacity

Most SMART GROWTH users have found that the capacity assessments can be done in clusters of four or five; and—in fact—all twelve should not be attempted in a single meeting or a brief retreat. It is just too much information! By focusing on a few capacities, the foundation can focus on priority concerns and can handle the "to-do" list that emerges from the analysis.

For example, a foundation concerned about the coherence and alignment of its strategies might choose to look at the capacities of grantmaking, direct programs, community role, impact/measurement, and values. The combined information from these five capacities will help a foundation better view its programmatic resources as they relate to these categories. The interconnections of programmatic resources will become clearer and the importance of impact measurement can be established.

A foundation concerned more about the effectiveness of its operations might choose board, staff, financial management, systems, planning, and values.

Public foundations that are raising pass-through funds while also building endowments, donor advised funds, and other partnerships might choose board, staff, financial development, marketing/communications, systems, and values.

Some foundations have used SMART GROWTH as the primary tool for an organizational audit, often as preparation for a milestone strategic planning process. An audit process is typically accomplished over several weeks or months. This time frame makes it possible for the organization to use all or most of the capacity assessments and to obtain a 360-degree view of itself—its progress, assets, and developmental challenges.

Individual and group use

An individual founder or leader can benefit from using SMART GROWTH—PF. This can be useful for a board chair, CEO, or department head who needs to gain some perspective or insight about the growth and development of their organization or team.

However, most SMART GROWTH users have found that it is most dynamic and comprehensive in a group setting where many individuals participate in all or part of the analysis. The value of many perspectives at once seems to lead to "truth-telling" in the organization. The value of "hive-mind," that is, many different minds focused at once on the issues, yields more understanding of more dimensions of an issue.

SMART GROWTH is designed for easy use within a regular board or staff meeting, or as the framework for a retreat. The Quick Quiz provides an ice-breaker for getting a rapid and approximate picture of the foundation's overall life stage and the capacity assessments can be used by the full group or divided for use by specific staff teams or board committees.

Self-help or consultant facilitation

Although designed as a self-help tool, SMART GROWTH seems to be a richer and more enjoyable process when it is facilitated by an outside organizational development consultant or coach trained in SMART GROWTH methodology. The reasons are straightforward. A consultant

- Spares the CEO or board chair the time needed to invent the process or create the setting in which SMART GROWTH can be used (though the CEO or board chair needs to work with the consultant).

- Enables everyone to participate because no staff or board person needs to hold him or herself out of the process to serve as the facilitator.

- Brings perspective that insiders lack. Often the consultant will see patterns and will be able to interpret results in a neutral and constructive way.

- Interprets findings, facilitates problem solving, and enables the foundation to set a new course for development by bringing professional background and the benefit of learning experiences with other clients.

- Synthesizes the findings from diverse teams into one unified picture for the organization.

- Helps the group or team to create a "whole out of the sum of the parts."

Success Stories

Staff and board members are hard working, dedicated to their organizations, and usually believe they have a good perspective on the organization. Yet the insider's view can become cramped and often suffers from laser-like concentration on single or disparate parts rather than a complete understanding of the whole.

Here are some examples of breakthrough insights resulting from actual SMART GROWTH assessments that, in turn, led to new and different actions to strengthen the organization.

- **An international foundation** wanted to use SMART GROWTH itself before sharing it with its grantee-partners (other smaller foundations) and also wanted to use SMART GROWTH to better understand a problem with its own fundraising process. The deeper capacity assessments revealed some expected strengths and weaknesses along with a gap in the strategic plan causing difficulties in making a compelling case for the foundation's new direction. The staff took a break from the SMART GROWTH process and returned for a day to the strategic planning process to modify and complete the plan. This yielded a new logic model that everyone could understand that, in turn, made the action steps and implementation inspiring for all.

- **A young city-based public foundation in the United States** was feeling the first signs of fatigue following an enormously successful start-up phase. In a four-hour session, a small staff (two people) and most of the board (fifteen members) built an understanding of the Stage 3: Grow and Deliver challenges that matched their own real experiences. They chose three capacities to focus their efforts on: fundraising, board capacity, and values. A reexamination of values helped to integrate new board members and inspire everyone to renew and strengthen their vision. The board recognized that it would need to remain strong and hands-on throughout Stage 3, especially in fundraising, to support an innovative and entrepreneurial (but tiny) staff. This abbreviated application of SMART GROWTH was enough to enable the organization to get past a transitional moment and to continue building the fund.

"We got a lot of good direction and information from the process. What an excellent model. It also does the trick in keeping board members 'focused' on the structure/mission of the organization."

— *Rosemary Mitchell, executive director, Women's Foundation of Genesee Valley*

- **A small but successful public foundation with an endowment** already in place, nearing Stage 4: Delegate and Evaluate, discovered through SMART GROWTH that its informal and intuitive sense of strategy was aligned with its broad vision but was not strategic enough to produce tangible outcomes. As a result of SMART GROWTH the foundation initiated a series of stakeholder dialogues and then worked through a strategic planning process to create a logic model to capture its strategic approach to grantmaking and programs, clarifying to itself and the community its intended outcomes. This also enabled all in the organization—including board members with admirable but personal agendas—to begin making decisions on the basis of strategy rather than on the feelings of members or the intuitive sense of how "right" something felt.

Frequently Asked Questions

Managing the expectations of users of an assessment tool is one of the most important keys to success. Like all participatory processes, the organization will get out of the experience what it puts in. However, many leaders secretly hope for a magic potion that will be quick, easy, and perfect, and therefore they expect SMART GROWTH to do all things for all problems. Sometimes leaders view all assessment and developmental processes with such cynicism and doubt that it is difficult to appreciate process—even when it works. In either case, the expectations are out of proportion to the realistic potential of SMART GROWTH.

Some of the most common questions about SMART GROWTH and about organizational development include the following:

- *Isn't our organization too* different *to benefit from a single or "packaged" model?*

  Regardless of differences and varying activities in grantmaking and operating programs or choice of strategies (charity, empowerment, systemic change, or other), public and private foundations have much in common. Most foundations share common developmental patterns in the areas of governance, staffing, grantmaking, planning, values, and impact measurement.

They *do* differ noticeably in the areas of financial management and resource development, as well as marketing or strategic communications, because private funds do not need expertise in fundraising and sustainability (other than investment strategies). Without the need to raise funds, the private foundations can afford—and most choose—to invest in administrative systems and technology, while public foundations often struggle to afford such infrastructure expenses. Those funds that live with larger entities like community foundations or national philanthropic institutions or federations are also often well supported with systems and technology, but it is more difficult to create an identity and fully express values—either in social change strategies or within larger organizational policies and procedures.

We feel that because SMART GROWTH relies on customization (through dialogue, reflection, and the expertise of a facilitator), the tool is universal enough to be trustworthy as a standard yet flexible enough to be highly individualized.

- *Does a foundation's age imply a larger size? Greater outcomes?*

In general, the largest public foundations (by grantmaking, endowment, or staff size) are also the oldest in chronological age and have the most advanced life-stage designation—or they are in a second or third cycle of development. A typical life stage for a public foundation created in the late 1980s or early 1990s would be a Stage 4, 5, or 6 life stage in the first life cycle. Public foundations created in the late 1990s and into 2001 are likely to be in Stages 2 and 3.

However, the circumstances of a public foundation's startup (for example, starting with an endowment or paid staff in the first stages) can yield exceptionally fast growth and development. Conversely, starting with very small donors—even a lot of them—will yield slower financial growth and therefore less grantmaking and influence.

Private foundations' developmental patterns cannot usually be correlated to size because endowment levels will be predetermined by the founder's or family's resources. However, small foundations that do not or cannot invest in staffing, consulting assistance, strategic planning, or impact measurement are likely to stay small.

- *Do all foundations develop at a similar pace?*

Yes and no. Most funds have a roughly predictable pace throughout the stages and the transitions between the stages. Most stages last between two to four years and most "between-stages" are twelve to eighteen months. But many funds are unpredictable, with a few foundations moving substantially faster or slower than others. Environmental factors, changes in the financial base, leadership transitions, and the degree of clarity (or confusion and discontent) about vision and values all will affect the speed of growth and effectiveness of the foundation. (See below: Are the life stages predictable in terms of time frame? And what accelerates and inhibits growth?)

- *Do all foundations find the same skills easy or difficult to acquire?*

No, not exactly. Distinct patterns of skill development appear at each stage of organizational life. For example, most foundations focus first on their board and the basics of giving gifts or grants, and in later stages add strategic communications, impact measurement, and so forth. And there are also patterns that follow the foundation structure (private or public, grantmaking or operating). But, many variables affect skills and capacities. For example, the strengths of an executive director or board member will affect how skills are acquired.

SMART GROWTH research has indicated that

- Across all the life stages, staff leadership is described as one of the easiest skills to acquire because funds can search and hire a person suited to their needs and professional staff bring skills and expertise with them.

- Grantmaking is described as easy by most funds . . . with the exception of those in Stages 4 and 5, the points at which the funds begin to add formal evaluation and look for tangible outcomes that are directly aligned to and supportive of vision and mission.

- Most foundations report that governance capacity is one of the most difficult capacities to acquire. Boards spend relatively little time together; they are bound together by vision but not necessarily by skills or style.

- Financial management and fundraising (for public funds) seem like easy capacities to attain during start up but difficult to sustain during growth.

- All foundations—public and private—report that attaining capacity in impact measurement is quite difficult.

- Young foundations usually find it difficult to master administrative systems, and mature funds often find marketing, strategic communications, and technology systems to be challenging.

- *Do life stages have a predictable time frame?*

No two foundations are alike as they move from stage to stage. In addition, time frames are difficult to predict with precision because some foundations move back and forth between two life stages before they summon the momentum and resources to completely shift into a different stage. For example, some public foundations have reported that setting goals for large endowment growth often requires substantial rethinking of staff structure, board fundraising strengths, and technology systems. Often these capacity areas are out of sync with the fundraising goals. These circumstances can lead to some back-and-forth movement between stages as the fund strives to set and reach ambitious new goals and is pulled back by lack of capacity.

At the same time there are predictable patterns, and these may be comforting to foundations questioning their intuition of being "stalled" or "speeding." For example, in Stage 2: Start-up and Launch, the founder or founding group is articulating the main vision and organizing a working group. This stage is marked by rapid progress that can last from six to twelve months. Yet despite this speedy pattern typical of Stages 1 and 2, some funders have spent years in the idea phase, and then after attempting a start-up they "fail" and fall back into a talking and planning phase. Overall, Envision and Commit (Stage 1) and Start-up and Launch (Stage 2) together usually take about two years.

The later stages tend to last longer (sometimes four to six years in each stage) because of their complexity; the transitions between stages are also longer. But some foundations will defy the rule.

- *What accelerates or inhibits growth?*

Funds that are moving fast—either in financial growth or in more sophisticated strategies—share the following early traits:

- Simply being a private fund can account for fast growth early on because the endowment is in place and staff and board have the resources they need to plan and implement ideas.

- Funds that reside inside large and supportive community foundations or federations enjoy some benefits that can accelerate performance, such as matching endowment support and staffing.

- An active and well-run board can be a huge accelerator, especially for public funds that need credibility and connections to raise endowments and annual funding.

Funds moving at a slow-growth pace often share the following traits:

- For public funds, a donor base that has mostly small donors and only a few major donors will inevitably have a slow-growth pattern. Small donors often have difficulty effectively reaching out to large donors; and small donors often are tempted to use a lot of their volunteer energy on small-scale events. While being committed to a "democratized" philanthropic base (donors of all sizes are welcome and are participating) is a great value to hold and is important for the long-term future, it slows down the pace of financial growth.

- Funds housed within community foundations can experience values conflicts and identity confusion that slow down the ability of others in the community to recognize what the women's fund actually stands for. While a fund of this type benefits from the name brand of the bigger entity (the community foundation), the name brand also makes it difficult for the fund to operate autonomously.

- The inability or unwillingness of founders to hire and support staff and to work cooperatively with a staff professional can slow growth and often create distrust or conflict that has to be solved before real growth can begin.

Fast growth—while attractive—is not the same as maturity and sustainability. Organizations that grow too fast are often daunted by the challenges of sustainability and the steady leadership and systems required for the long haul. Entrepreneurial skills that serve the start-up process can undermine needed stabilization.

At the same time, slow growth does not guarantee maturity. Slow growth organizations can be hampered by too little entrepreneurial zest and innovation, leaving them lackluster in style and unable to create irresistible and positive ties to donors and other growth partners.

Lessons Learned

Following are some of the best lessons others have learned from SMART GROWTH.

- *Hire and trust an executive director.* A foundation that tries to operate too long with either family volunteers or founder-volunteers risks too much informality in both style and substance.

- *Unleash creativity through trust.* Philanthropy is ultimately a relationship-building process. Establishing values and behaviors that reinforce the presence of a trusting culture where new ideas can be expressed and explored will reinforce a high level of creativity.

- *Good systems and growth go hand in hand.* An increasing volume of work along with confusing and ad hoc systems can eventually break people and organizations. Ad hoc decision making undermines trust and the ability of the organization to be strategic. Lack of appropriate technology and procedures can result in administrative chaos; neither staff nor board can meet expectations for productivity without the appropriate flow of information. Broken or inadequately small systems can destroy trust.

- *Hire for the future . . . not the past.* Often organizations are tempted to hire significant leaders who match requirements for what the foundation "used to be." This means that the person is likely to do the job appropriate to the past—not the future. Without going overboard, the foundation should try to "hire up" to the stage it wants to be in the near future.

- *Make time for regular reflection and assessment of the organization.* The process should be blame free, but don't be afraid to hold each other accountable.

Board and staff retreats, reviewing the flow of evaluation and feedback, and facilitated dialogue are all examples of steps organizations can take to learn and grow.

- *Engage board and staff in assessment.* Their perceptions about the organization are inevitably different because of different daily experiences and perspectives of the organization's work.

- *Revisit vision and values frequently.* Transmit organizational and mission values each time the composition of staff and board change.

Summary

Life-stage assessment provides a context for a foundation's current challenges and facilitates plans for growth and development. Foundations considering an assessment or review process should also consider these practical aspects of the process:

- Make a starting "guess" about whether you see the assessment process as major (180 degrees) or minor based on apparent needs. For example, a major organizational change such as a merger, sudden expansion or contraction, or significant leadership change might require a major assessment process, while a "tune-up" of a good and relevant strategic plan and most other things holding steady would only require a minor assessment process.

- Review SMART GROWTH and consult the resource materials to find other assessment tools that might suit your needs.

- Talk to your organizational development consultant (if you have one), your executive coach, or a board member with organizational development skills to decide whether the process should be facilitated. (Most major processes will require facilitation.)

- Set some specific goals for what you want to learn in an assessment.

- Set a budget consistent with the goals and invite facilitation proposals (knowing that you may need to adjust your budget as well as your assumed commitment of time by staff and board).

- Consider how you plan to use the information uncovered in the assessment. Will it flow to the staff management team? To the board? To a planning committee?

- Strike a balance between a bit more than you think you want to do and a bit less than the board or a consultant may advise. You cannot and will not ever get the answers to all your questions. You will need to continue running the organization with improved but still imperfect information!

For more information about the SMART GROWTH tools, please visit http://www.wfnet.org.

Conclusion

by Carol Lukas and Sandra Jacobsen, Fieldstone Alliance

The tools described in this book vary greatly both in their objectives and design, and the examples provided here represent only a small fraction of the variety of tools available. (A more comprehensive, but not exhaustive, list is available in the Appendix.) For grantmakers new to capacity assessment tools, the stories in this book might raise as many questions as they answer. Here are answers to some obvious questions grantmakers might have.

- *Where do I go from here?*

  As expressed in the introductory chapter, success with capacity-assessment tools relies on clear goals and objectives and open communication with grantees. If your organization is thinking about using a capacity-assessment tool, use the considerations laid out in Chapter 1 as a discussion guide to help you decide what you hope to accomplish with a such a tool. Also, grantmaking board and staff members should consider assessing their *own* capacity as a first step—using the Grantee Perception Report, the SMART GROWTH tool, or another capacity assessment tool—before assessing grantees' capacity.

- *How do I decide which tools are more appropriate in our situation? How do I go about modifying tools to suit our purposes?*

  After you have identified your objectives, start looking at various tools to see which ones fit best with what you are hoping to accomplish. You'll find that it is an iterative process—as you look at the possibilities each framework or tool offers, you'll expand your ideas about the goals you can or cannot achieve.

Note that unless you've been trained in organization development or a related field *and* have significant experience, this process might be akin to an untrained person trying to build an automobile by reading an assembly manual. It is complex, requiring both general knowledge about how organizations function, and specialized knowledge in *all* functional areas of organizations (governance, leadership, organizational structure, program design and impact, human resources, finance, marketing, and risk management, to name a few). Most funders find that they need to hire an expert to help them in the planning stage.

Figure 9, Comparison of Nonprofit Capacity-Assessment Tools (page 184), compares the assessment tools described in this book and may help you make some initial decisions about your organization's design criteria.

- *How can I get these tools?*

Some of the tools described in this book are available on the enclosed CD-ROM. These are only a small portion of the different types of capacity-assessment tools available. Unfortunately, no published index lists all assessment tools in existence. The Appendix gives a listing of some assessment tools and resources; others can be found by surfing the Internet; scanning books on organization development or organization effectiveness; or talking to peers, consultants, or management support providers.

- *Who can help us with assessment?*

If you're not sure how to proceed, or are feeling overwhelmed by the complexity of choices, you're not alone. Many funders who start to wade into these waters find that they need an expert advisor or consultant to help them craft their strategy and make design decisions. Luckily, many people have devoted their careers to studying and practicing organization assessment.

You can search for consultants with experience in organization assessment in a variety of ways.

- Ask other grantmakers that have started assessment programs who they've used, and how effective that person's assistance was.

- Check with local management support organizations or intermediaries to see if they have staff or consultants with expertise in organizational assessment.

- Many cities and regions have online nonprofit consultant directories that list areas of expertise; in some you can even search for "organizational assessment." Check with your local nonprofit association or management support organization to see if such a directory exists in your area.

- The Alliance for Nonprofit Management, the professional association of individuals and organizations devoted to improving the management and governance capacity of nonprofits, has a searchable directory of nonprofit consultants and management support providers. They list more than 250 individuals and organizations across the country that assist with organization assessment.

It goes without saying that you need to do due diligence in hiring any consultant or resource person to help you with this. Be sure to find out if they not only have experience conducting assessments, but also designing assessment programs.

Whether you decide to collaborate with other grantmakers or go it alone, use an already existing tool or create a new one, capacity-assessment tools can have powerful potential. Using them on your own organization or with your grantees can help illuminate problems or inefficiencies that may have otherwise gone undetected and can often be a springboard for improved effectiveness and expanded impact.

Figure 9. Comparison of Nonprofit Capacity-Assessment Tools

	McKinsey Capacity Assessment Grid (SVP Version)	*CapMap®*	Unity Foundation C.Q.® Capacity Quotient
Functional Areas	1. Mission, vision, strategy and planning 2. Program design and evaluation 3. Human resources 4. Senior management team leadership 5. Information technology 6. Financial management 7. Fund development 8. Board leadership 9. Legal affairs 10. Marketing, communications, and external relations	1. Board governance 2. Community connections 3. Executive director 4. Financial management 5. Fund development 6. HR & staff development 7. Management information systems 8. Real estate asset management 9. Real estate development	1. Advancement capacity 2. Leadership capacity 3. Treasury management capacity 4. Operations capacity
Number of Questions	61	Approximately 30 per module	75
Time to Complete	About 1 hour	About 2 hours per module	35–45 minutes
Suggested Respondents	Executive director, board member, 1–3 staff members	LISC staff interviews staff leading each capacity area and board members for the board governance module	All executive staff and all board members. 100% participation is required in order to obtain a Benchmarks Report
Top Line or In-depth?	Top Line	Top Line	Top Line
Self- or Third-Party-Administered?	Self-administered	LISC program staff collaborate with staff and board members	Self-administered
Used for Funding Decisions?	No	No	Yes
Primary Goal	Build grantee capacity and develop a portrait of capacity across grantees or a field	Build grantee capacity	Build grantee capacity

	Mary Reynolds Babcock Foundation Tool	**Grantee Perception Report**	**SMART GROWTH**
Functional Areas	1. Management/ Administration 2. Finances/ Fundraising 3. Governance/Board 4. Program 5. Human resources 6. Evaluation 7. Communications 8. Technology	1. Assessing foundation-grantee relationships on a comparative basis 2. Assessing grantmaking strategies/impact on a comparative basis 3. Assessing foundation performance on a comparative basis 4. Providing operational benchmarking data	Life Stages: 1. Envision and commit 2. Start-up and launch 3. Grow and deliver 4. Delegate and evaluate 5. Specialize and control 6. Renew and rebuild Capacities: 1. Planning 2. Programs 3. Grantmaking 4. Resource development 5. Financial management 6. Systems 7. Marketing and strategic communications 8. Staff 9. Board/Governance 10. Values 11. Community relationships 12. Impact/Measurements
Number of Questions	N/A	50 questions directed at grantees	Each capacity has its own set of questions Quick Quiz: 12
Time to Complete	N/A	30 minutes	20 minutes per capacity assessment Quick Quiz: 15 minutes
Suggested Respondents	Assessor interviews staff, board, and stakeholders	Full fiscal year of active grantees	Appropriate staff for capacity assessment/all staff and board for full assessment (all capacities) Quick Quiz: One person or entire staff/board
Top Line or In-depth?	In-depth	Both	Full assessment (all capacities and comparison of ratings): In-depth
Self- or Third-Party-Administered?	Third-party-administered	Third-party-administered	Self-administered
Used for Funding Decisions?	No	N/A	N/A
Primary Goal	Build grantee capacity	Enhance grantmaking and assess foundation performance	Enhance grantmaking

Organizational Assessment Resources

BoardSource: Board Self-Assessment Tool

This full-board self-evaluation questionnaire enables board members to examine and improve board performance. The instrument is based on research related to key characteristics of effective boards.

http://www.boardsource.org

Center for Effective Philanthropy: Grantee Perception Report®

Provides foundation CEOs, boards, and staff with data on their foundation's performance on a variety of dimensions relative to a selected peer group. For more information, visit

http://www.effectivephilanthropy.org/assessment/assessment_gpr.html

Development Training Institute: Leadership Self-Assessment Tool

Competency assessment for community development organizations covering management and financial areas.

http://www.dtinational.org/training/tools/assess.asp

Drucker Foundation: Self-Assessment Tool

This participant workbook and process guide helps nonprofits address four questions: Should the mission be revised? Who is the primary customer? What are our results? What does the customer value?

http://www.pfdf.org/leaderbooks

Fieldstone Alliance: Nonprofit Life Stage Assessment

Places a nonprofit organization in one of five life stages relative to seven organizational domains—governance, staff leadership, financing, administrative systems, staffing, products and services, and marketing. The entire assessment is included in Judith Sharken Simon, *The Five Life Stages of Nonprofit Organizations: Where You Are, Where You're Going, and What to Expect When You Get There* (2001). The assessment only is available as a free, online service at

http://surveys.wilder.org/fieldstone/lifestages/

Fieldstone Alliance: Organizational Assessment Guides and Measures

Includes performance standards for community development corporations for the six components of organizational capacity referred to in this book. Phone: 651–556–4500.

Harvard Business School: The Balanced Scorecard

Developed by Harvard Business School professor Robert Kaplan, the Balanced Scorecard incorporates performance measurements related to finances, how constituent needs are being met, and how a nonprofit organization is delivering on its mission.

http://www.hbsp.harvard.edu

InnoNet: Self-assessment Instrument

Offers comparative analysis of assessment tools and their use for different subject areas and groups. Field-tested.

http://www.innonet.org

Local Initiative Support Corporation: *Cap*Map®

Designed to assist LISC program staff in mapping the current capacity of an organization, working in partnership with a CDC to determine a path for growth and measuring success along the way. More information is available at

http://www.lisc.org/winston-salem/assets/asset_upload_file969_4552.pdf

The Management Center: Nonprofit Assessment Tool

Eight-part, eighty-item online assessment tool intended to help organizations measure their capacity and performance in administration and leadership, board of directors, community relations and marketing, finance, human resources, planning, program, and plant and equipment.

http://www.tmcenter.org/

Mary Reynolds Babcock Foundation

Foundation conducts its own in-depth capacity assessments of grassroots grantee organizations. For more information on the Babcock Foundation, visit

http://www.mrbf.org

Maryland Association of Nonprofits: Standards for Excellence

Enables peer reviewers to measure performance for standards related to mission and program, governance, human resources, financial and legal, fundraising, and public affairs.

http://www.mdnonprofit.org

McKinsey & Company: Capacity Assessment Grid

Assesses seven broad areas of capacity, with specific indicators under each category. Customized by several grantmakers. Available online at

http://www.vppartners.org/learning/reports/capacity/assessment.pdf

National Civic League: The Civic Index

A twelve-part self-assessment tool to help communities evaluate and improve their civic infrastructure—the interplay of people and groups through which decisions are made and problems are resolved at the community level.

http://www.ncl.org/publications

The Nature Conservancy: Resources to Success

Designed for nongovernmental organizations, this organizational assessment tool provides indicators for eight categories of nonprofit functioning. The booklet includes guidance on how to conduct an organizational self-assessment.

http://www.publications@tnc.org

Neighborhood Progress, Inc.: Mapping the Road to Excellence: Operating Guidelines for Community Development Corporations

Assessment tool covering legal, financial and budgeting, human resources, governance, planning, IT, communications, and program management areas. Available in distance learning program.

http://www.neighborhoodprogress.com

Women's Funding Network: SMART GROWTH

Life-stage assessment for grantmaking organizations. Includes a quick quiz and a more in-depth assessment component. For more information, visit

http://www.wfnet.org/documents/smartgrowth.pdf

Unity Foundation: Capacity Quotient (C.Q.®)

Online assessment board and staff members take individually for a comprehensive reading of organizational capacity. Nonprofits can also apply for funding or register for capacity training from the Unity Foundation. For more information, visit

http://www.unityfdn.org/cq.html

Index

c indicates chart
f indicates figure
t indicates table

More results-oriented books from
Fieldstone Alliance

Funder's Guides

Community Visions, Community Solutions
Grantmaking for Comprehensive Impact
by Joseph A. Connor and Stephanie Kadel-Taras

Helps foundations, community funds, government agencies, and other grantmakers uncover a community's highest aspiration for itself, and support and sustain strategic efforts to get to workable solutions.

128 pages, softcover   Item # 06930X

A Funder's Guide to Evaluation: Leveraging
Evaluation to Improve Nonprofit Effectiveness
by Peter York

This book includes strategies and tools to help grantmakers support and use evaluation as a nonprofit organizational capacity-building tool.

160 pages, softcoverItem # 069482

A Funder's Guide to
Organizational Assessment
Tools, Processes, and Their Use in Building Capacity
by Grantmakers for Effective Organizations

Describes 4 grantee assessment tools and tow tools for assessing foundation performance. You'll learn how each tool was developed, what its features are, how it's used, and lessons learned from leading practitioners.

216 pages, includes CD-ROM   Item # 069539

Strengthening Nonprofit Performance
A Funder's Guide to Capacity Building
by Paul Connolly and Carol Lukas

This practical guide synthesizes the most recent capacity building practice and research into a collection of strategies, steps, and examples that you can use to get started on or improve funding to strengthen nonprofit organizations.

176 pages, softcover   Item # 069377

Collaboration

Collaboration Handbook
Creating, Sustaining, and Enjoying the Journey
by Michael Winer and Karen Ray

Shows you how to get a collaboration going, set goals, determine everyone's roles, create an action plan, and evaluate the results. Includes a case study of one collaboration from start to finish, helpful tips on how to avoid pitfalls, and worksheets to keep everyone on track.

192 pages, softcover   Item # 069032

Collaboration: What Makes It Work, 2nd Ed.
by Paul Mattessich, PhD, Marta Murray-Close, BA, and Barbara Monsey, MPH

An in-depth review of current collaboration research. Major findings are summarized, critical conclusions are drawn, and twenty key factors influencing successful collaborations are identified. Includes The Wilder Collaboration Factors Inventory, which groups can use to assess their collaboration.

104 pages, softcover   Item # 069326

A Fieldstone Nonprofit Guide to
Forming Alliances
by Linda Hoskins and Emil Angelica

Helps you understand the wide range of ways that they can work with others—focusing on alliances that work at a lower level of intensity. It shows how to plan and start an alliance that fits a nonprofit's circumstances and needs.

112 pages, softcover   Item # 069466

The Nimble Collaboration
Fine-Tuning Your Collaboration for Lasting Success
by Karen Ray

Shows you ways to make your existing collaboration more responsive, flexible, and productive. Provides three key strategies to help your collaboration respond quickly to changing environments and participants.

136 pages, softcover   Item # 069288

For current prices visit us online at 🖥 **www.FieldstoneAlliance.org**

Management & Planning

The Accidental Techie
Supporting, Managing, and Maximizing Your
Nonprofit's Technology
by Sue Bennett

How to support and manage technology on a day-to-day
basis including setting up a help desk, developing an
effective technology budget and implementation plan,
working with consultants, handling viruses, creating a
backup system, purchasing hardware and software, using
donated hardware, creating a useful database, and more.

176 pages, softcover   Item # 069490

Benchmarking for Nonprofits
How to Measure, Manage, and Improve Performance
by Jason Saul

This book defines a formal, systematic, and reliable way
to benchmark, from preparing your organization to measuring performance and implementing best practices.

112 pages, softcover   Item # 069431

The Best of the Board Café
Hands-on Solutions for Nonprofit Boards
by Jan Masaoka, CompassPoint Nonprofit Services

Gathers the most requested articles from the e-newsletter,
Board Café. You'll find a lively menu of ideas, information, opinions, news, and resources to help board members give and get the most out of their board service.

232 pages, softcover   Item # 069407

Consulting with Nonprofits: A Practitioner's Guide
by Carol A. Lukas

A step-by-step, comprehensive guide for consultants. Addresses the art of consulting, how to run your business,
and much more. Also includes tips and anecdotes from
thirty skilled consultants.

240 pages, softcover   Item # 069172

The Fieldstone Nonprofit Guide to
Crafting Effective Mission and Vision Statements
by Emil Angelica

Guides you through two six-step processes that result in a
mission statement, vision statement, or both. Shows how
a clarified mission and vision lead to more effective leadership, decisions, fundraising, and management. Includes
tips, sample statements, and worksheets.

88 pages, softcover   Item # 06927X

The Fieldstone Nonprofit Guide to
Developing Effective Teams
by Beth Gilbertsen and Vijit Ramchandani

Helps you understand, start, and maintain a team. Provides
tools and techniques for writing a mission statement, setting goals, conducting effective meetings, creating ground
rules to manage team dynamics, making decisions in
teams, creating project plans, and developing team spirit.

80 pages, softcover   Item # 069202

The Five Life Stages of Nonprofit Organizations
Where You Are, Where You're Going, and What to
Expect When You Get There
by Judith Sharken Simon with J. Terence Donovan

Shows you what's "normal" for each development stage
which helps you plan for transitions, stay on track, and
avoid unnecessary struggles. Includes The Nonprofit Life
Stage Assessment to plot your organization's progress in
seven arenas of organization development.

128 pages, softcover   Item # 069229

The Lobbying and Advocacy Handbook for Nonprofit Organizations
Shaping Public Policy at the State and Local Level
by Marcia Avner

This book is a planning guide and resource for nonprofit
organizations that want to influence issues that matter to
them. This book will help you decide whether to lobby
and then put plans in place to make it work.

240 pages, softcover   Item # 069261

The Manager's Guide to Program Evaluation:
Planning, Contracting, and Managing for Useful Results
by Paul W. Mattessich, Ph.D.

Explains how to plan and manage an evaluation that will
help identify your organization's successes, share information with key audiences, and improve services.

96 pages, softcover   Item # 069385

The Nonprofit Board Member's Guide to Lobbying and Advocacy
by Marcia Avner

Written specifically for board members, this guide helps
organizations increase their impact on policy decisions. It
reveals how board members can be involved in planning
for and implementing successful lobbying efforts.

96 pages, softcover   Item # 069393

For current prices visit us online at www.FieldstoneAlliance.org

The Nonprofit Mergers Workbook
The Leader's Guide to Considering, Negotiating, and Executing a Merger
by David La Piana

A merger can be a daunting and complex process. Save time, money, and untold frustration with this highly practical guide that makes the process manageable and controllable. Includes case studies, decision trees, twenty-two worksheets, checklists, tips, and complete step-by-step guidance from seeking partners to writing the merger agreement, and more.

240 pages, softcover   Item # 069210

The Nonprofit Mergers Workbook Part II
Unifying the Organization after a Merger
by La Piana Associates

Once the merger agreement is signed, the question becomes: How do we make this merger work? *Part II* helps you create a comprehensive plan to achieve *integration*—bringing together people, programs, processes, and systems from two (or more) organizations into a single, unified whole.

248 pages, includes CD-ROM   Item # 069415

Nonprofit Stewardship
A Better Way to Lead Your Mission-Based Organization
by Peter C. Brinckerhoff

The stewardship model of leadership can help your organization improve its mission capability by forcing you to keep your organization's mission foremost. It helps you make decisions that are best for the people your organization serves. In other words, stewardship helps you do more good for more people.

272 pages, softcover   Item # 069423

Resolving Conflict in Nonprofit Organizations
The Leader's Guide to Finding Constructive Solutions
by Marion Peters Angelica

Helps you identify conflict, decide whether to intervene, uncover and deal with the true issues, and design and conduct a conflict resolution process. Includes exercises to learn and practice conflict resolution skills, guidance on handling unique conflicts such as harassment and discrimination, and when (and where) to seek outside help with litigation, arbitration, and mediation.

192 pages, softcover   Item # 069164

Strategic Planning Workbook for Nonprofit Organizations, Revised and Updated
by Bryan Barry

Chart a wise course for your nonprofit's future. This time-tested workbook gives you practical step-by-step guidance, real-life examples, one nonprofit's complete strategic plan, and easy-to-use worksheets.

144 pages, softcover   Item # 069075

Finances

Bookkeeping Basics
What Every Nonprofit Bookkeeper Needs to Know
by Debra L. Ruegg and Lisa M. Venkatrathnam

This book will enable you to successfully meet the basic bookkeeping requirements of your nonprofit organization—even if you have no formal accounting training.

128 pages, softcover   Item # 069296

Coping with Cutbacks:
The Nonprofit Guide to Success When Times Are Tight
by Emil Angelica and Vincent Hyman

Shows you practical ways to involve business, government, and other nonprofits to solve problems together. Also includes 185 cutback strategies you can put to use right away.

128 pages, softcover   Item # 069091

Financial Leadership for Nonprofit Executives
Guiding Your Organization to Long-term Success
Jeanne Bell Peters and Elizabeth Schaffer

Provides executives with a practical guide to protecting and growing the assets of their organizations and with accomplishing as much mission as possible with those resources.

144 pages, softcover   Item # 06944X

Venture Forth! The Essential Guide to Starting a Moneymaking Business in Your Nonprofit Organization
by Rolfe Larson

The most complete guide on nonprofit business development. Building on the experience of dozens of organizations, this handbook gives you a time-tested approach for finding, testing, and launching a successful nonprofit business venture.

272 pages, softcover   Item # 069245

For current prices visit us online at www.FieldstoneAlliance.org

Marketing & Fundraising

The Fieldstone Nonprofit Guide to
Conducting Successful Focus Groups
by Judith Sharken Simon

Using this proven technique, you'll get essential opinions and feedback to help you check out your assumptions, do better strategic planning, improve services or products, and more.

80 pages, softcover   *Item # 069199*

Marketing Workbook for Nonprofit Organizations Volume I: Develop the Plan
by Gary J. Stern

Don't just wish for results—get them! Here's how to create a straightforward, usable marketing plan. Includes the six Ps of Marketing, how to use them effectively, a sample marketing plan, tips on using the Internet, and worksheets.

208 pages, softcover   *Item # 069253*

Marketing Workbook for Nonprofit Organizations Volume II: Mobilize People for Marketing Success
by Gary J. Stern

Learn how to mobilize your entire organization, its staff, volunteers, and supporters in a focused, one-to-one marketing campaign. Comes with *Pocket Guide for Marketing Representatives*. In it, your marketing representatives can record key campaign messages and find motivational reminders.

192 pages, softcover   *Item # 069105*

ORDERING INFORMATION

Order by phone, fax or online

Call toll-free: 800-274-6024
Internationally: 651-556-4509

Fax: 651-556-4517

E-mail: books@fieldstonealliance.org
Online: www.FieldstoneAlliance.org

Mail: Fieldstone Alliance
Publishing Center
60 Plato Boulevard East, Suite 150
St. Paul, MN 55107

Our NO-RISK guarantee

If you aren't completely satisfied with any book for any reason, simply send it back within 30 days for a full refund.

Pricing and discounts

For current prices and discounts, please visit our web site at www.FieldstoneAlliance.org or call toll free at 800-274-6024.

Do you have a book idea?

Fieldstone Alliance seeks manuscripts and proposals for books in the fields of nonprofit management and community development. To get a copy of our author guidelines, please call us at 800-274-6024. You can also download them from our web site at www.FieldstoneAlliance.org

Visit us online

You'll find information about Fieldstone Alliance and more details on our books, such as table of contents, pricing, discounts, endorsements, and more, at www.FieldstoneAlliance.org.

Quality assurance

We strive to make sure that all the books we publish are helpful and easy to use. Our major workbooks are tested and critiqued by experts before being published. Their comments help shape the final book and—we trust—make it more useful to you.